Wicked Official

MAINE DICTIONARY

By
Bonnie Sullivan Millett

Published by True Beginnings Publishing.

ISBN-13: 978-0692822449
ISBN-10: 0692822445

Ordering Information:
To order additional copies of this book, please visit Amazon or contact the publisher at: true_beginnings_publishing@yahoo.com for bulk orders.

This book is a work of non-fiction. All people, events, incidents, and dialogues are portrayed and accurate to the best of the Author's ability. Some names have been changed to protect the innocent. All of the writings and musings of this book are part of the Author's personal experiences and are copyrighted to the Author and protected under US Copyright law. The purpose of this book is to record and share the Maine ways, sayings, and dialect with the world.

Wicked Official Maine Dictionary.
© Bonnie Sullivan Millett.
First Printing 2017.
Printed in the United States of America.

This book is dedicated to my
precious parents in Heaven:
Evelyn A. and Clarence "Nick" Sullivan.

Many, many thanks to my dear friend,
Linda Churchill, for all her help.

Wicked Official
Symbols

 **Stands for Wicked Official**
(similar to a bird flying up from the sun)

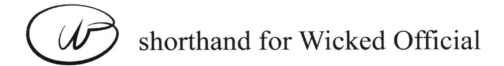 shorthand for Wicked Official

Wicked Official Maine Dictionary

Table of Contents

Introduction

Do you, for whatever reason, want to find out what it's like to talk like a Mainer – especially a Down East Mainer? Well, here's the book you can count on to do just that. You will sound like <u>and</u> be able to understand the real locals as well as understand the words that have a special meaning for the Maine people. After all, without clear communication, you can get in a wicked bind. That is to say, a lot of trouble.

People of all kinds are just great. The better we get to know and understand one another, it only enriches our lives. This book is aimed specifically at bringin' people closer together – by better understanding one another and sharing experiences. I hope you have a great time doin' just that.

For some Mainers there is that "uh–oh" feeling that occurs when "people from away" come up. That's not altogether a bad thing. After all, people are different. But we are all human beings, the majority of us more good than not. As part of this diversified group, I feel an obligation to do what I am able to help bring us closer together with understanding, if not empathetic tolerance. Hopefully, each of us can maintain an individual pride of our heritage AND maintain the peace. Is more compassion too much to hope for? Definitely not!

There's too much in this life that's just not fun. This book is especially for people everywhere who never get enough fun–or maybe don't even know how. Readin' this publication will help jog loose that hidden funny bone that's stuck somewhere inside you. Jar that thing! Wake it up! You'll likely get more than you're bargaining for.

There's also a romantic fiber involved here, since Mainers are naturally tied to the basics of life – love, liberty, fun, honesty (as much as necessary to keep things simple and straight forward,) and hard work. <u>Got</u> to have humor to survive with any sanity and general tolerance of things. Laughin' at yourself can be more cathartic than grandma's sulfa and molasses.

Readin' this book lets you take a little trip (without leaving home) into what it would be like to have the mindset of a Mainer–especially a Down East Mainer. I hope you enjoy yourself and don't feel badly if you get the feeling that you missed something. You pro'bly did. But it's nothing you can't figure out by readin' between the lines and lettin' your mind go. After all, comin' to Maine has a way of makin' all the fuss, fluff, and useless parts of life fade away. You become more aware of your real self and what's important to ya. What you do with that insight will be your choice. May God bless ya, heart and soul.

If you want to get really picky about where Down East starts, it is very formally said to begin at the mouth of the Penobscot River where it empties into Penobscot Bay at Bucksport, ME and continues east to the Canadian border. However, many consider the state of ME, especially coastal Maine as Down East.

Oh! No! I almost forgot to commend the people of Boston for keeping their accent alive. They are music to my ears. They and the Maine accent are definitely cousins. I wish you all the best. Go Boston! Boston Strong!

Please don't think for a minute that I have any intentions of puttin' down any of the other treasured accents you'll find in this great country of ours. Take the laidback southern accent, for example. A southern belle could charm the boots off a jockey with a well spoken, sugar sweet, smooth southern accent. I'll never forget what my Aunt Angie (Uncle Jim's wife on my father's side) told me when I was just 13 years old.

There happened to be a naval ship in the harbor for the 4th of July, and Uncle Jim, Angie, and family were up visiting from MA. It came evening time and my older sister, Susan, wanted to head downtown (we were in Bar Harbor) where the action was. But she didn't want to go alone, so she asked me to go with her. (She must have been desperate). I was reluctant and very naïve. Aunt Angie came off the front porch to where Susan and I were on the sidewalk. I was draggin' my feet but finally agreed to go down town. Angie came up to us and told us, "You girls look out for all those sailors." (Susan's eyes were just dancing.) "Especially look out for those southern boys," she said. "They can be very charmin', especially to you young girls." I was skeptical about leavin' but Susan was more eager than ever – so off we went.

As I said earlier, I've never forgotten Aunt Angie's warning. It is so true. There are few things more charmin' than a southern gentleman. That southern accent... it too must be preserved – as does that heart-warmin', downright home lovin' Texas twang. It can entertain or even be adorable, dependin' on the delivery.

We can't forget, either, the curt, no nonsense accent of the died–in–the–wool New Yorker. They are real attention getters, from the Long Island, all business touch, to the down to earth accent of the Bronx – no foolin' around. They are unforgettable. Yes, we need to find a way to preserve all our priceless treasures.

The Maine accent is playful, yet very practical. My goal is to preserve this precious gem of sociology for our ears and our hearts. Speaking of sociology, that brings to mind a man called Ignatius Donnelly. He lived 11/03/1831 to 1/01/1901. He was born the son of an Irish immigrant, Philip Carrol Donnelly, who settled in Pennsylvania, PA.

Mr. Ignatius Donnelly became a man of many accomplishments. At a prestigious high school, he excelled primarily in literature and became a lawyer. He became an object of scandal and moved to the Minnesota Territory, where he became Lt. Governor, then Congressman, then on to being a state senator (a

Republican). He was also an early supporter of women's suffrage. He returned to his law practice in 1878 and resumed his writing. By 1882 he published "Atlantis; The Antedeluvian World". But it's his sociological studies that caught my interest. He studied language and especially the English dialects. He made the following statement: "Anyone who has observed the wide divergences between the pronunciation of English as spoken in the United States, in England, in Australia, or in South Africa (in the period preceding talking pictures and radio) will have realized that without some such means of standardizing speech, another 200 years would have sufficed to render the speech of various English speaking groups unintelligible, the one to the other. This goes to show that without some stabilizing influence, the English language as we know it, would have vanished."

Along the same vein, I certainly don't want the Maine, especially the Down East Maine dialect to become extinct. And it will unless there is some source of catalogin' it. That's <u>exactly</u> what the Wicked Official Maine Dictionary is all about – preserving the Maine dialect.

Like any social development, language has its hows and whys that made it into good solid tradition. A tradition (until now) that has probably never been so specifically identified and catalogued. The Wicked Official Maine dialect has always been passed on from one generation to another. But if dialect is to survive, it's time to document it before it's eaten away by the increasing number of "imports" (that is, people from away). More constant exposure to the way others talk is having an impact on the Maine dialect. Southern Maine, especially, is already affected. Hopefully, this book will provide more of a stumbling block and slow down the impact so many people are having.

Reading about the Maine sayings, facts, and humor lets you take a tiny trip (without leaving home) into what it would be like to have the mindset of a Mainer. I hope you enjoy yourself.

When you get to the Wicked Official Maine Dictionary, itself, I have yet to hear professional actors or comedians do the Maine accent accurately. They could certainly benefit from this book.

The last section is the Wicked Official Down Eastah Test. It doesn't take long to find out how close you come to being a Wicked Official Down Eastah. So – sit back. Get comfy. Have some fun and enjoy this rare, special aspect of our country.

About the Author

I, Bonnie Ellen Millett, was born Bonnie Ellen Sullivan in 1949 on Mount Desert Island in Bar Harbor, Maine. My father, Clarence "Nick" Sullivan, was born and raised in Bar Harbor as well. His father, George Washington Sullivan came from Gouldsboro, ME, across Frenchman's Bay to Mount Desert Island and settled in Bar Harbor as a young man. His father, William Sullivan, had brought his family to Gouldsboro from Prince Edward Island, Canada. William's family had come to P.E.I. from County Cork, Ireland. They were O'Sullivans. The family dropped the "O" to become Sullivan when they came to the good old USA.

My Father's mother, Blanche Dodge Sullivan, was from a long line of Down Eastahs, especially from Tremont and Pretty Marsh on Mount Desert Island. My mother, Evelyn Arlene Sullivan, was born in Weeks Mills, ME in 1917. She was a Plummer. Her father, Stephen Plummer was born there, too. His people came to Weeks mills from Plymouth, ME. My mother's mother, May French Plummer was born in Summersville, ME. My lineage is documented and was told to me by my mother on November 19th, 2011.

The point I'm making here is that just by heritage and generations of exposure to the Maine way of life, it qualifies me as more than capable and somewhat of an authority on Maine people, their way of life, habits, and traditions. I have been a keen and tireless observer of Mainers simply because I love them and am very proud of them. I'm proud of who I am as part of this precious, hardworking, earth and sea loving, inventive group of people who would do anything to help their fellow man, especially any Mainer.

I have always loved people, all kinds of people. This was part of the motivation for starting this book. My goals are to promote the understanding of Mainers and help everyone get along better in doing so. Also, I've always been a stickler for detail. It really irked me to hear people try to speak the Maine dialect, especially Down East Maine, and get it SO wrong! But how were they to know? The dialect has always been just passed along from one generation to another.

I decided to take it upon myself to catalogue and document the Mainer's way of speaking – for a number of reasons: 1) If anyone really wanted to speak as a Mainer, there would be a place to go to reference that information. 2) If anyone wanted to better understand the way Mainers talk and what they mean, that would be covered as well. 3) To, hopefully, slow down the gradual fading away of the accent. 4) To bring Mainers and people from away to a closer understanding AND to share some little-known humor and facts about Maine. I'm not saying I've covered it all, but I've put a pretty good dent in it.

The Wicked Official Maine Dictionary is one great way to break down barriers and reduce ignorance. Ignorance is worse than being unarmed at a fly swatting contest in June. And in June you get every kind of fly there is comin' at ya. The person who came up with the saying, "Ignorance is bliss" must be trapped somewhere in La–La–Land – definitely not in the real world.

If you have a feeling for people in general, goodness, and the lighter side of life, see what a great time you can have playing around with this Wicked Official Publication. What your mind comes up with might surprise ya, enlighten ya, and for sure (pronounced shoo–uh) will be wicked good for ya. This advice coming from me – a practicing RN for over thirty four years.

There are two more things to let you know "About the Author". 1) The strong faith in Almighty God is and has been a dominant force in my life ever since I was a toddler. The love, strength, and guidance I have received from this all powerful, loving force has been such a complete blessing. I don't always understand, but I'm absolutely sure my life would be missing SO MUCH without this spirit. I cannot put into words just how grateful I am and how much love has been generated. 2) MUSIC! From the Irish songs we sang as a young family on St. Patrick's Day (and throughout the year) to the glowing Christmas carols and songs in church – music has been a thrilling, joyful part of my life.

From the old country/western songs of Roy Rogers and Gene Autry (with that beautiful yodeling) to the deep, melt your heart tunes of Josh Turner, ALL the music from the 1950s, '60s, and many of the '70s to the more modern artists of today such as the Backstreet Boys and Taylor Swift. From the solo trumpet to the full orchestra, it's all so movin'. And when I was able, I never missed a chance to dance. My heart always pounds with the National Anthem and tears flow with the theme songs of the military, along with John Philip Sousa's moving creations.

I want to thank my precious sisters and brother for all they've done to help make me who I am. Sister Susan, bright, brave, able to tackle any challenge and come out on top. Brother Dan, courageous, mysterious, always protective of me – there for me and I for him. Joan, my baby sister. She is deterred by nothing. She is a cowgirl at heart, and we share a lot of hopes and dreams. Sue, Dan, and Joan, I love you and thank you for being there for and with me.

I must thank my precious son, Llewellyn Andrew Sullivan of whom I'm extremely proud. He has been very supportive of me and my attempting this project. Hopefully, I WILL accomplish this before the dialect disintegrates like Aunt Anne's old lace-trimmed hanky.

At this point I give you my deepest gratitude for looking into this unique publication – and wish you lots of fun while exploring it. If you enjoy this book, you may also enjoy the history and stories in my other book, "Growing Up on Mount Desert Island MAINE". May God Bless You, always.

Facts – about Maine and Mainers

1) Late summer 2013, the "Live with Kelly & Michael" show came on. What Kelly had to say really "stuck in my craw", so to speak. She voiced her opinion on how long Christmas decorations should continue on display in the State of Maine. She went on to say that "there should be a national law that says all Christmas decorations are to be taken down by January 14th of the following year." Well, Kelly, if you're offended by Christmas decorations staying up – then Get Over It! What is it to you anyway?

You don't have a clue what is involved when it comes to Christmas decorations in Maine. It has gotten pretty cold in Maine by the time decorations are put up. God bless the stout-hearted Christians who go through the effort it takes to put up a nice display. If it is really cold, icy, slippery, and snow-covered by mid-January (and it usually is), it just doesn't take much common sense to figure out that it's not worth the exposure, discomfort, and in some cases, danger that is involved in taking the decorations down. Besides, some people enjoy the festive, attractive look, and downright fun in keeping the decorations up. It is each person's individual right to do as they please in this situation, as well it should be. If you take offense, Kelly, then just don't look!

I actually like the Kelly and Michael Show, generally…but this time, Kelly stepped over the line. As of February 10th, 2017, Kelly announced she still has her Christmas lights up and just might keep them up year-round. You go, girl!

2) I mean, if you can't appreciate the unique perfume of the mudflats, it's not your nose that's broken.

3) Sure, you like rabbit stew, as long as someone else kills the rabbit.

4) The only thing that makes an experience better is to share it.

5) Don't go wading in the mudflats unless you have time to get stuck, especially if the tide is comin' in.

6) Take a shortcut only if it's worth what you'll miss along the way.

7) Wicked good – it can't get any better than wicked good. It's the ultimate – the very best.

8) Pudge – describes someone or something who is pudgy (chubby), but pudge is not in Webster's 4th Edition. The word/name brings to mind a good ole local guy who was nicknamed Pudgy back in high school, (Rick Delaittre). Of course, he outgrew that.

9) You look forward to a town meetin' like a blue fish feedin' frenzy on a school of mackerel.

10) Gnarly – a slang term – for Wicked Official purposes, it is occasionally used, mostly by younger folks, to mean something is "very cool", a good thing.

11) Fart – a slang term with two meanings. 1) the expulsion of flatus (gas from the rectum – pronounced faht). 2) someone who is uncooperative, stubborn, has a negative outlook, not nice.

12) Old Fart – less negative then a younger fart. It brings to mind someone of the male gender who is over the age of 60 and isn't very cordial to most people AND doesn't rush to get things done, mostly 'cause he doesn't give a shit.

13) Frig – One word my dad was fond of using was "frig", not friggin' so much, but he was quick to use "frig". It usually was something he didn't feel like doin' – because it was too much of a frig (a hassle, a bother, or just not doable with the amount of ambition he possessed at the time). Oh, by the way, you won't find the words "frig" or frigging" in Webster's – 4th Edition.

14) Wicked Good Things: The Red Sox, The Boston accent, huntin' (that's with or without killin' something'), playing with your kids, the ring/dong of a bell buoy, the Patriots, unconditional love, a forgivin' police person, playing with your pet(s), Fort Knox (the one just beyond Bucksport, ME), a shiny car that can go fast, The Boston Bruins, Aroostook County's ('The County') hills and open fields, U. of ME Black Bears, Thunder Hole, The Red Sox, a family picnic, Big Sand Beach, The Great North Woods (they cover part of Northern Maine, N.H., VT., N.Y., and then part of Quebec – collectively 26,000,000 acres), fishin', Bailey's Irish Crème, Acadia National Park, The Carriage Roads, and Drop-Kick Murphy's. Hurray and five cheers for the fantastic Champion New England Patriots!!!!! Five timeSuperbowl winners!

15) Enth degree (not found in Webster's). When someone has done something to the "enth degree", they have done their level best to accomplish their ambition – tried as hard as humanly possible to meet that certain goal. The enth degree is the ultimate in measure or assessment. It was one of my mother's favorite expressions.

16) Cha Ching. This word makes me think of money, especially when quite a profit is involved. You see, the old-fashioned kind of cash register would make a "cha ching" sound whenever the cash drawer was opened, indicating a profitable transaction had probably (or you could say "probly") just took place.

17) Bugger (pronounced Bug-uh) – this is a term with a dual meaning. A bugger can be a problem, very hard to solve – such as when you get a flat tire and the lug nuts just won't come off. That's a real "bug-uh". Also, a bugger can be an adorable small child. Example: after Sam got covered in mud while playin' with his trucks, Uncle Pete saw him and said, "Isn't he a cute little bug-uh."

18) Would you believe that only Maine wood can be burned in Maine? It's true. The Maine Legislature banned ALL out-of-state firewood. Wood "from away" can carry harmful diseases and insects into the State.

19) There are some very small measures used by many Maine people in general. All I can do is tell you what those tiny amounts mean and how they are in relation to one another. We won't get into infinitesimal. It is not in Webster's, but Urban dictionary describes it as "an amount approaching zero". It would be pretty much useless to most people.

My mother taught me to cook using the standard measures (cups to spoonfuls) plus the following smaller measures when called for. Mom had been taught to cook by her mother, passed it on to me and made me a good "down home cookin'" woman. My son picked up what I knew and became a good cook in his own rite. But he added knowledge of holistic healthy cooking with quite a variety of spices.

The following measures are listed in order of largest amount to smallest.
- **a)** bit – a very small amount but more than a pinch.
- **b)** pinch – the amount one can pick up between a thumb and finger.
- **c)** smidgen – Webster's calls this the same as a bit. I don't believe this. If it was true, why bother using the word smidgen. In my cooking, a smidgen is definitely smaller than a bit.
- **d)** dite – not listed in Webster's. When I use a dite of something, it's nothing more than a crumb or two.
- **e)** iota – If you have an iota of something, it's next to nothing. Example: One day a fellow (known to stretch the truth at times) told me he would pay back the $20.00 I had lent him. Well, I didn't believe him, one iota.

20) Would you believe almost 2/3^{rds} of the population in the United States cannot see the night sky due to manmade light sources? Not so on most of Mount

Desert Island and much of Maine. Especially in Acadia National Park, you have numerous panoramic views of the fabulous night sky. There is even an annual Acadia Night Sky Festival.

21) The last fact is prob'ly the most important to list. What makes a person a REAL local? After talking with a number of locals, the consensus was unanimous. No matter how well a person fits in with everybody, no matter how much a person contributes to the town, no matter how much of a local accent they have, no matter how much someone may love the land, sea, mountains, etc, no matter if you are married to a local, no matter if you have children born here, no matter if your parents or other relatives were born here, no matter how many years someone has lived here, if you were not born here, you cannot be considered a local. It may sound hard hearted, but a line has to be drawn somewhere. (Still, if it was up to me, but of course it's not, I'd love to call Jeff Dobbs a local.)

Images

1) Anyone who claims you don't have enough sense to get out of the rain has never been gently, tenderly kissed on the lips on a spring day in the middle of a warm, soft rainy downpour. Thank you G.M. RIP

2) Imagine you just walked out of a stand of fragrant pines to find a sun-drenched meadow with the sweetness of fully bloomed milkweed being stirred by a gentle breeze and dotted with monarch butterflies.

3) The fragrance of the lilacs begins to fade as you notice the return of the mother robin, once again, to feed her hungry offspring. The eager youngsters chirp and shove, hoping to be first to get the tasty tidbit. The air begins to stir as you hear the thunder of the approaching shower. Time to move along.

4) Holding hands, you and your love walk barefoot across the sand at mid-tide. You look back to see your footprints. The gulls are watching as they wait for the tide to go out. The fresh salt air seems to be moving the white puffs of clouds across the blue sky. The color nearly matches that of the ocean. Almost heaven.

5) Sittin' with your dog on the huge rocks that go down to the ocean. The sun grows warmer as you feel the gusty northwest breeze blowing just enough to keep you cool. Your eyes grow a bit drowsy and you feel like humming a tune. Just how happy can one person get?

6) A driving south east wind writhing waves with green foamy brine. That special monster wave is rolling closer, closer – then BOOM!!
It plunges into the craggy cavern. THUNDER HOLE. Spray-soaked smiling people all the way to the road. Your smile can't leave your face and the exhilaration can't be duplicated. AND you know it.

7) You made it to the top of Cadillac Mountain and choose to rest on the western ridge to watch the sunset. The ridge was freckled with curious onlookers full of excitement and anticipation. As you wait for the sun to descend and the colors begin to erupt, you take in the panoramic, breathtaking view of lakes, forests, mountains, and in a distance, the ocean. The blue sky with clouds just above the horizon, begins to turn to yellow – then gold. As the sun continues to seep below the earth, the vivid reds and scarlets overpower the entire western sky. With the shades changing, the clouds take on a golden florescent glow along their base. Only God can make such a delight. The colors gradually fade and high areas of darkness begin to reveal the occasional twinkle of the night sky. You continue to sit, watching the horizon, hardly able to absorb all you have seen from your panoramic perch. Then Look! The North Star.

8) We walked along the rocky shore together – delighted to find ancient tide-washed bottles, as well as broken colored glass. After climbing the cliffs, we rested in the fragrant orchard. The sun was warming, and the delicate breeze felt soft across our skin. Sensuous lips seeking one another as we laid cushioned among thick green grass. Everything was fresh and young, and so were we.

9) You find yourself almost holding your breath to prevent makin' the slightest sound that might disturb the calm of standing on the Carriage Roads at the quaint sign post that points you to Eagle Lake, to the right, or up to the top of Paradise Hill, to the left. There isn't a single man-made smell or sound. The only things you hear are the song birds calling to one another – and the little gurgling stream on its way to join Duck Brook and move on down to Frenchman's Bay. But the smells – Oh, those delicate whiffs on the breeze as they bring you the fragrances of the evergreens and the sun-drenched pine needles. You wait quietly, hoping to see a squirrel, a chipmunk, or even a deer. But – not today. Your eyes did get to feast on the shapes and colors of the trees, boulders, mosses, plants and sky, along with the perfumes that can only be produced by the magic of such nature.

10) Sunshine is warming your face, arms and legs. You take your shoes off and deeply inhale the cool, moist, salty air that comes drifting across the cold, deep blue ocean. Watch the waves roll onto the shore as you curl your toes into the soft, warm sand. Because it's only 10 in the morning, the beach isn't too hot – yet.
Sea gulls begin their serenade with their unique half chirp, half squawk-like sound, as they swoop toward the crest of the waves. People are coming carefully over the large, gray granite steps. The steep walkway aids inquisitive visitors to reach the gorgeous, expansive cove. Lobster fishermen tend their traps offshore. Tourists pass high above the cliffs on Ocean Drive.
Ah, ah, ah – resting back on your towel to view the puffy white clouds as they drift across the endless sky.
As the sun rises more, the water sparkles and waves dance over the sand and rocks. It calls to you to test the water. Slowly acclimate as you get knee deep

– far enough! Then stand on the shore in shallow water and feel the retreating waves draw the sand from beneath your feet, tickling.

Time to look for unique shells and pebbles, but the tide is too high, hiding most of the treasures. Oh, well – another time. But the sun is high now – perfect for a sun bath before finally leaving Big Sand Beach in Acadia National Park. How fortunate AND blessed I am to have lived so close to such glorious creations.

11) Ahh – Otter Cliffs – an overlook that has a drastic plunge from the road straight down to the base of the cliffs, where the ocean meets the shore.

Whether you're there during the day to see the panoramic, glistening deep blue ocean with the islands in a distance – OR at night in the pitch darkness with only the moon reflecting beams across the bay, there is always the lonesome bell buoy forever keeping its post. Warning! Warning! The boats of the ledges. CLANG! It sounds, as the waves toss the giant buoy like a toy.

When the sea is calm, you have to wait to hear the mournful tone that has a slight echo in the quiet. When the sea is agitated and churning, the waves keep rising, tossing, surging at the big heavy buoy like a toy, and forcing the bell to toll with urgency. Warning! Warning! Those near and far of the dangers below.

NOTE: The next three images will have a completely different tone. They are true occurrences, actual interactions between and among the local folk of the Mount Desert Island area. The language as well as the images are somewhat risqué – which is not at all unusual among "the locals".

12) One day not long ago, my red-headed, horse-loving, younger sister, Joan, decided to go down the road a piece (about 2 1/2 miles, or so) to visit with the fella who owns the lot of land where the infamous fire of 1947 started. She was interested in buying some of the land (mostly bog, now – cranberry bog). Dave, Joan's significant other (and my ex-husband) went along with Joan to visit Bob. They had a great visit, chewin' the fat about a number of things. Eventually, the conversation came around to sex, as it often does. Bob asked Joan if she had ever heard of Tapioca – lived over on the back side (meaning the southwest side of Mount Desert Island – some call it the "quiet side"). Jo said she never heard of her. "Well", said Bob, "a guy could go over and have her in a minute – so they call her Tapioca".

13) One day the (so-called) black sheep of the family came in and told me he had run into one of my friends downtown – that they met-up in one of the local snack bar/gas stations purely by accident. (He was not especially fond of her, to put it mildly.) She said to him, "Hello," just to be social. He told me he turned around, saw who it was and said to her, "Are you talking to me, Bitch?" She made no response. He went on to say to her, "If you ever speak to me again, I'll rip your head off and Sh** down the hole!" This is shocking but true.

By the way, a Mainer doesn't have to be the black sheep of the family to get foul or offensive. I must say, the above encounter was shocking to me. (It made our black sheep laugh!)

14) The following is a true story about a piece of Bar Harbor's history. Some of the names have been changed to prevent offending anyone or anyone's family.

Of course, there is always a favorite bar or hang out in most Maine towns. They often change every generation, or so, except for the few that go on for several decades (often family-run businesses). In Bar Harbor in the 1950s and earlier, it was the bars at Testa's, Tripps, and the infamous Green Door.

There had been a place on the west side of lower Main Street, not far from the town pier, in the 1950s that was called Toulleo's. It was a family-type restaurant and hang out where parents could take their children for hotdogs and sandwiches. I remember my dad taking us kids to Toulleos's on Saturdays for a soft drink of some kind after our routine family outing in Acadia National Park. We hiked Carriage Roads, climbed mountains like the Bee Hive, the Bowl, Dorr's, and some I don't remember the names. He usually got us a bag or two of fresh popcorn, to go. It was often more than just us Sullivan kids. Neighborhood friends would often go with us. What fun! Dad, having grown up in Bar Harbor, knew all the great places to go.

Times changed and a man from the Bangor area, named Ron Hitchcock came, and Toulleo's disappeared. Fortunately for us, we had "outgrown" a family-type restaurant anyway. By the 1960s and 70s the area where Toullio's had been turned into shops and Rooster's Cellar. There had been multiple other smaller business that helped occupy the area. In general, the west side of Main Street – but none as outstanding as Rooster's Cellar. Of course, there was a street level "upstairs" part of Rooster's, as well, but it was Rooster's Cellar that was the place to go for a good time.

Anyone even close to 21, and up, would land at "The Cellar" just as soon as they got out of work. If you didn't work, you landed there, too. What a crowd. It was like one big extended outrageous family. It wasn't just locals, either. People from away usually didn't have any problem fittin' right in. Many came off the cruise ships, too. It was just a magnet for a good time.

On street level, Clarence Silk's plumbing shop was a bit south of "the Cellar", and Super Sandal's (Mike Ross') leather shop was just downhill from it, closer to West Street.

Anyone could hear the music coming from the juke box as they passed by. It was loud enough to draw people from the other side of the street and Agamont

Park. Popular tunes like Carole King's "I feel the Earth Move", The Doors, The Rolling Stones, The Who – you name it. It was a home away from home and LOADED (no pun intended) with pals.

The restroom had a life of its own, too. When they were not occupied for "nature calls", you might find some good ole fashion hanky panky, new fashioned tokin' up, or just plain getting some privacy for some other reason.

There were very unique, memorable, local souls who almost made "the Cellar" a second home. There also seemed to be bar people and booth people. The booth people were good about keeping the juke box going – but could be the origins of a number of scuffles, too. The bar people were mostly just interested in drinkin' and scoutin' out for a possible companion or two for the night. The bar was a very sociable place, and the bartenders sort of kept the peace.

'Bout the time things are just as fun as anything could possibly be, this is when the gal nicknamed "Mattress Matty" and at least one of her gal pals would show up. Sometimes, she'd get there earlier and be a major instigator of good ole fashion jokin' and dancin' – yes, dancin'. Her age was anybody's guess, was barely 5 ft. tall, and always with that big toothless grin. If anyone could round up a partner or two for the night, Matty definitely could. And she loved to dance so much she didn't even need a "paht-nuh", just a good mood.

Matty often settled down a ways on the west side of the bar with one of her close pals like Carley Trout, or " Big" Dotty Heathers. Of course, Matty's "main man" was Allen Morton. What stories could be told! Allen saw Mike one day and asked if he had seen Matty. Allen showed Mike a big sack of "lob-stahz" and said he was huntin' for Matty "to get me some".

My best pal and I would often sit in the "Cellar", usually at the bar. We each kept a beer going to wet our whistles and every so often, she would have a shot of tequila and I would have a shot of cognac – just to keep things interestin'. We would usually sit just to the left of the mid bar and wonder about our future. You see, Matty's frequent companion was Carley. My pal and I would wonder which of us would be like Matty and which would be like Carley in about 40 years; Matty with her toothless grin and Carley with her quirky hair. We creeped ourselves out after a while and didn't stay on the topic for long.

Matty had had quite a life. During WWII, when the Naval Vessels came in the harbor with sailors hungry for more than food and drink, good ole Robert Cummins could count on Matty helping him meet the "boy's" needs. Robert also owned the big motel right on Main Street and that Matty worked on commission. She was some memorable character AND the life of any party.

Back to Rooster's Cellar: My pal and I sat at a booth, sometimes with other friends. Lindsy Dogins comes to mind. What a sweetheart. It wasn't long before she became Lindsy Marks – married to Rob Marks, the eldest of the Marks brothers. They made a beautiful pair. God love her. She passed <u>far</u> too soon.

You never know just who would come through the door of Rooster's Cellar and set up their own particular type of mischief. So many wonderful locals would come in like some different kinds of spices and all join together to create a <u>fine</u> "dish". On any given night, you would likely find as many "imports" as there were "locals". Spontaneous activities could be anything from a fist fight (all for "fun") to a sensuous, spur of the moment strip tease. Those of you who were there know just who I'm talkin' about.

Some of those happy, lovable folks aren't with us anymore. If they only could know how much they are missed. But, there are also many memorable folks who are still with us, thank God.

God bless the patience and tolerance of Mike ("Super Sandal"). The leather shop porch abutted the entry way to Rooster's Cellar. He was amazingly patient and tolerant of all the "activity".

As they say, all good things must come to an end <u>and</u> times change. Sometime in the early 1970s, or so, a "local boy" (that is, he grew up in Bar Harbor, moved away, then returned) made his presence known in Bar Harbor. He returned a top notch black belt Karate expert and didn't take any guff from anyone. Well this fellow, Gerald Mitchell, bought Rooster's Cellar and the whole building involved. He made the "Cellar" into a gift shop, upgraded the restaurant, and made it into quite a respectable place, with Geddy (Gerald's nickname) at the helm and help from some very wise friends.

I had known Gerald and his shy, younger brother Louis just from growing up in the same small town. I knew Gerald as a quiet, kind, gentle, considerate guy who had a bit of a stutter at times. He also had a crush on my older sister, Susan. He always treated me with kindness and respect.

He publicized "Geddy's" and made it into a respectable place. Gone were the days of the old "Rooster's Cellar". Geddy's restaurant continues to this day, a fitting tribute to him, as he passed away a "couple" of years ago. What do you suppose the next metamorphosis will be? RIP G.M.

So much has changed in Bar Harbor over just the last 5 or 6 years. With big money having come in, the whole face of the wharf area and West Street are completely different. Gone is old Roger Cunningham's hotel on the corner of Main St. and West St. The actual building had become a decent restaurant called the Quarter Deck with rooms above rented out. Now it is gone, completely. Gone are the quaint shops and private homes that had been there even before the big fire in 1947. Now it's all money, money, money. What will be, will be.

15) To finish this portion on Maine images, I just have to fill you in on some treats of Southern and Northern Maine. It's easy to get carried away telling about Maine's many attributes and forget the primary purpose here of translating everyday American English into the Maine and Down East Maine Dialect.

There are beautiful, fun-filled attractions all over Maine – from one end of the coast to the other – from the sweeping sands and thrills of Southern Maine's Old Orchard Beach and the marvelous Sabago Lake to Northern Maine's Moosehead Lake, where the scenery is breathtaking and serene like nowhere else. Northern Maine also has elegant, 5259 ft. Mount Kahtadin. The colorful peak dominates the horizon for miles around. It is 133 miles beyond Bangor. But if you're headed toward Northern Maine via I-95, you can get a fantastic view of it if you watch off to the left, about 2/3rd the way to Houlton, from Bangor.

There are at least 100 miles beyond Houlton to the Canadian border. Aroostook County, the northern-most county in Maine, is full of wide open green fields, hills, as well as forests and potato fields

If you were to go Down East from Bangor, it would take about one hour and forty-five minutes to reach Calais, on the Canadian border. That's taking the direct route over pretty good roads. Of course, the coastal route would take much, much longer – full of great coastal towns and villages.

It doesn't matter where you go in Maine, you'll have such a memorable experience, and you'll find you can only return for more.

Sayings

1) **"Bug-uh (bugger)"** – This is a term with a dual meaning. A bug-uh can be a problem hard to resolve, such as when you get a flat tire and the lug nuts just won't come off. (Then you have to go find some "liquid wrench".) Also, a bug-uh can be an adorable, small child – as in the case when Sam had been playing with his trucks in the dirt and got dirt on his face, as well. Uncle Pete saw him and said, "Isn't he a cute little bug-uh?!"

2) **"Spooge"** – A term that covers a variety of substances. It is usually an unpleasant, gooey, sort of slippery and mucky stuff that needs to be cleaned up.

3) **"T'would"** – This is a combination of "it" and "would". It's just a Down East way of shortening the communication. Example: A person asks a Wicked Official Mainer if his woodstove's supply of kindling' could use some more. The man replied simply, "T'would", instead of a more lengthy reply such as, "My supply is low and I would appreciate having some more."

4) **"'magine"** – Here we have a word trimmed just to shorten the idea they are conveying. Example: A person was telling a W.O. Mainer about the new car their neighbor just bought – like how pretty it is, how fast it goes, how comfortably it rides, how well it handles, and how shiny it is. The W.O. Mainer replied, "'magine." (Rather than, "I imagine.")

5) **"Naw t'all"** – The gardener really appreciated the cold lemonade the cook brought to him one blisterin' afternoon. He thanked her profusely. She replied, "Naw t'all." She was saying, "not at all", meaning it was no bother at all.

6) **"'parently"** – This is a shortening of the word apparently. You would likely hear this reply in a situation similar to the following: A man has been waitin' for a fella to come look at the truck he has for sale. It was getting' quite late in the day and his wife mentioned that she didn't think the fella was goin' to show up. The man said, "'parently." He went on to say, "He don't know asshole from appetite anyway." (This last sentence has two things common

to the Mainer:)

   a) Sayin' "don't" instead of doesn't. I don't know just why this occurs. I do know it doesn't have anything to do with their knowledge of correct English, in most cases. It's simply habit.

   b) The man also used the sayin' about not knowin' "asshole from appetite". This is a commentary on the person's intelligence and amount of common sense. Basically, the fellow is not too bright and has little, if any common sense.

7) There are two words that quite often take the place of "anyway". One is "enuh -way" and another is "iny-way". No special reason, ya just hear it around (or even use it yourself)!

8) "Stinkpot" – This is a simple motor drive boat. Unlike a sailboat, it usually has an offensive odor from the gas or diesel fuel.

9) "'bout" – This takes the place of sayin' "about" or "it is about". This is just another way to reduce the number of words you need to convey an idea. Example: A person was tellin' the Mainer of their experience of acquirin' a new clothes washer. He described how the sales person finally came down to a reasonable price and plans on deliverin' it tomorrow. The Mainer replied, "Good! 'bout time." – using as few words as possible to convey his thoughts.

10) Have you ever heard of someone "<u>so</u> poor they can't even pay attention?"

11) The Saying Goes – "He has just one foot in the dorey." That's a foolish and precious position to be in, since a dorey is a small, flat-bottomed boat that tips over easily. This implies that either the guy doesn't know what he is doing or maybe doesn't realize his precarious position. Maybe, he's not "all there", as when someone is "one sandwich short of a picnic".

12) The Saying Goes – "He was "up the creek" (sometimes called a "crick") without a paddle." This guy is in quite a predicament because he was in a creek (or "crick"), also called a stream. It is trouble enough to be up a creek, but to be without a paddle too, is really bad, as he would need a paddle for propulsion and steering. That he was in a creek to begin with means the boat was something small, light, and drew little draft, like a canoe or kayak. That he was <u>up</u> the creek one could surmise that he had planned to go even further up the creek. Of course, that would be impossible without a paddle. At any rate, this person has several problems to solve.

13) "It's a hard row to hoe." – meaning that the task at hand is going to take a lot of effort and hard work to reach your goal. The saying came from when farmers actually hand-hoed a row of soil in order to plant their crops. It could even involve digging out sizeable rocks and roots that are in the way. I actually heard a fellow once say that someone had a hard <u>road</u> to hoe. (It was a comment made on People's Court 2/17/1998. He missed the point of the old saying completely!)

14) Some advice is to "nip it in the bud". – That is to say, stop the problem before it grows into a full-blown predicament. There is a fellow who has used the saying "nip it in the butt" for years. I wonder what in the world he means.

15) Someone was advised to "make a bee line" to the store, before the sale was over. A bee line is to cover a distance in the shortest route at a rapid pace, as a bee does when its goal is to return to the hive to report a good, new source of nectar (for making honey). I once heard a fellow refer to someone making a "B" line. Whatever could he have meant?

16) He "doesn't have both oars in the water." – This isn't literally about a man having oars in the water. It is figurative. It's referring' to his mental state as bein' less than "normal", not payin' attention and not knowin' enough to <u>put</u> both oars in the water in order to go where he wants. This fellow is quite handicapped, lackin' common sense. He's definitely missin' something and certainly NOT a problem solver.

17) "The Lights are on but there's nobody home." – This refers to a person who appears to be alright, when actually they're not alright at all. They don't seem to be aware of their situation and not likely able to figure it out. You probably have met people like this. It is hard to reach them. They look alright enough, but start up a conversation and you'll soon find a major deficit in being able to express him (or her) self coherently, combined with lack of common sense. They are much like someone who doesn't "have both oars in the water" – but worse – because they <u>appear</u> to be alright.

18) I can't tell you how many times my dad would come in the house after cleaning the snow and ice from the car and truck (-10 F, wind 30 miles per hour) and say, as he was rubbing his hands together, "It's colder than a witch's tit." One can only imagine just how cold that might be.

19) A friend came to visit one day as I finished writing out checks to pay some of the bills. She asked how I was doing. I told her, "I might as well be shovelin' shit against the tide." In other words, it felt like a continuous and endless endeavor.

20) Ron went to the garage one day to find his visitor had accidentally scratched the new paint job on the 1979 Corvette. "You maggot!" exclaimed Ron. I

think the definition here of "maggot" is self-explanatory.

21) "I'll show you just where the bear went through the buckwheat!" This situation is referring' to someone who has been obnoxious or offensive and you don't want them around. At any rate, they are not welcome and about to be told or shown just where they can go, possibly even with some physical assistance!

22) "The pot callin' the kettle black." – This is talking 'bout one person (the pot) that has just accused another person (the kettle) of being offensive, when the first person (the pot) is actually as guilty (if not more so) of the same sort of offenses as "the kettle". In other words, the pot is "the same color" as is the kettle but doesn't recognize this (or is not willing to.)

23) "Well, hello! (pronounced hullo) You ole bastard, (pronounced "bah stud") you!" – Even though the word bastard oft has a negative derogatory connotation, it's not uncommon for Mainers, especially men, to use it as a friendly greetin', especially if they haven't seen each other for quite a while.

24) "Out of the fryin' pan, and into the fire." – This is a situation where things haven't been goin' very well, in general. Then, not necessarily due to their fault (though some poor judgment may be involved) things get a lot worse. So, they were in a "hot" (uncomfortable) situation to being with – then, instead of things improving', things got a lot worse. (They ended up in the fire.) Again, poor judgment comes into play here.

25) "You hit the nail right on the head." – This means that you have accurately said or done what was needed to make the point dead on or accurate.

26) "Mad as a wet hen." – You would have to know hens (chickens) to appreciate just how upset one gets if it gets wet. Hens aren't very bright, in general (there are exceptions as with the pet hen my nephew, Lucas, had) and can be quite mean to each other – especially newcomers. So, if a hen gets mad, and gettin' one wet will do this, you are lookin' at one difficult, cantankerous, and possibly aggressive critter. They are capable of inflictin' a mean peck (that draws blood) and their toenails can be sharp weapons, too. Best stay well away from a wet hen OR don't get 'em wet to begin with!

27) "Make do." – This sayin' in Maine is as common and as sure as one day leads to another. Mainers learn early to improvise in many, various situations to accomplish a goal. It may not be the best way, the finest way or the easiest way, but it <u>will</u> accomplish the goal. It will "make do".

28) If someone isn't "playin' with a full deck", it means they are mentally and/or

emotionally challenged. It would not be fair to hold this person accountable for what they do or say. They're just not responsible –no judgment, although they can be a very friendly, funny, harmless, and likeable person.

29) "He doesn't have the brains God gave a goose." – Far from a compliment, this is quite a putdown. A goose is so stupid that often it won't even sit to lay an egg. They have pretty long legs, too. It's not unusual to find one egg has broken – too bad, as they are delicious and nutritious. To say something good about a goose – they are very loyal and protective of their territory. <u>Don't</u> piss one off, that is, make it angry or aggravate it. You'll be sorry. They do make very observant and protective companions.

30) Some locals, especially older locals, have been known to play with a tourist's mind. The following is one example: A tourist was driving along the coast of Maine, just sightseein'. he ended up in Prospect Harbor, totally lost. he looked up the road and saw an old codger, by the looks, and thought "ah, a local!" He drove up to him in high hopes he would get directions back to the main highway. When he asked the man for directions, the man looked at him, hesitated a moment, scratched his head and simply said, "You can't get there from here."

31) "Man, I'm dryer than a popcorn fart!" – This is just lettin' someone know how thirsty you are.

32) "Oh! My achin' ass!" – This is an expression of exasperation. The person's literal rear end is not achin'. It's just an expression that conveys just how fed up they are with the situation. Somethin' needs to change. (And you can bet it will!)

33) "You don't know shit from shinola!" – This is not a compliment by any means. It is accusing the person of being so stupid that if they were to be assigned the task of shinin' some shoes, they wouldn't know one substance from another. It's 'bout the same as sayin' "you don't have the brains God gave a goose" – OR they just said something totally unbelievable and is bein' told he doesn't know what he's talkin' 'bout.

34) "Oh, go piss up a rope." – Here there are at least two people present and one is very annoyed by the other, and they just want the one being annoying to leave – go <u>any</u>where – just leave, even if it's to go do some useless or impossible task.

35) Another use for the phrase "go piss up a rope". One person may have told another person something that's unbelievable. That person may be told to "go piss up a rope", about as possible as the other fellow is asking him to believe.

36) I'm so tired, "I don't know if I can make it from pillar to post." – Back in the day, granite pillars (not very big – maybe 3 ft. tall) were used as markers for property lines, fences, driveways, and decoration. To make a continuous fence line or to mark the beginnin' or end of somethin', wooden posts were added. These two types of markers were not very far apart. So, if a fellow was <u>so</u> tired that he wasn't sure that he could make it from pillar to post, it would be a good idea that he not even try. Maybe he should sit for a while and hope a ride would come along.

37) "He's (or She's) lower than a gutter snipe." – One can't get much lower than that, unless maybe whale shit.

38) Saved for those that are so despicable, "they waste air when they breathe." "You piece of shit!"

These two statements can be a come-back to someone who has just asked a stupid question with an obvious answer – or someone so full of themselves that they are barely tolerable.

39) Does a chicken have teeth? One of those "duh!" questions to which the answer is obvious. NO, a chicken doesn't have teeth. (Not countin' the "egg tooth".)

40) Does a bear shit in the woods? Another one of those "duh!" questions. <u>Of course,</u> a bear "goes" in the woods. When someone asks you a "stupid" question, you can answer back with such a question. A dear friend (more of a family member), Paul Crowley, is a great one to use this type of response. He has an incredible sense of humor.

41) "Finest Kind" – Used to indicate strong admiration or special attraction to an especially nice person or situation.

42) "Hard tellin', not knowin'" – It's hard to tell what the truth of a situation is if you don't <u>know</u> to begin with.

43) "Hey, Chummy" – If you're called a "Chummy" by someone, it's very complimentary, indicating a closeness and that you are fondly respected.

44) "Ā-uh" – Used in the place of "yes", "most likely", or "I agree". (Shoo-uh or Shō-uh – sure).

45) "Yes-suh" – It has more emphasis than just "yes" or Ā-uh. ("Yes, sir!")

46) "Wicked Good" – Any word that has "wicked" prefacing it indicates profound emphasis on that word. If the word "wicked" is used alone, it indicates strong emotion toward the situation. It can be good or bad, depending on the situation.

47) Whenever it rains out of a clear, sunny sky, it's "the devil licking the hand of his Creator". In other words, the impossible is happening.

48) "Tougher than tripe." – When anyone would eat a cut of meat that was hard to chew, it wouldn't be uncommon for them to exclaim, "Tuf-uh than tripe!"

49) "You old biddy." – It takes the place of using a cruder name when you want to call someone a name but not be really offensive.It infers the person is picky and quarrelsome – generally not a very nice person.

50) "Prob'ly" – This takes the place of "probably" 99% of the time.

51) "Happy as a clam at high tide." – You can only get clams at low to half tide, so when it's high tide, the clams are totally safe, therefore happy.

52) "Holy cat turd!" – This is an exclamation that would be used when you have some sort of negative, unexpected outcome. You're spending time with an unexpected male visitor when, surprisingly, your boyfriend shows up. That's when you would exclaim, "Holy cat turd!"

53) "Crazier than a bedbug." – A bedbug really doesn't have a brain. It's just a useless parasite that lives to suck blood out of people. Because it's so brainless, it's actually crazy, and its craze is to get blood. Bedbugs have no common sense and no purpose in their action except to draw blood and mate. They're a useless being that moves around aimlessly.

54) "More useless than a fart in a mitten." – This saying refers to anybody who is supposed to know how to do their job but they don't. They don't retain the training they've been given, so they're very useless. Correspondingly, they are as useless as a fart in a mitten. A fart has no purpose and no function, at all, in a mitten, not even to warm your hands. To be as useless as a fart in a mitten is about the lowest, most useless thing you can say about anybody.

Wicked Official
Maine Dictionary Preliminary

Words that are pronounced in Maine the same way as in the rest of the country will not appear in this book. There would be no point. Words like cake, apple, and lewd would just be taking up pointless space. I must confess that there are some words in the dictionary that I have never heard a Mainer say – such as "a posteriori". This will not be appearing in the Wicked Official Maine Dictionary, either.

At this point, you need to be made aware of an idiosyncrasy of the Way Down East (abbreviated in the key as WDE) people – especially coastal folk and fishermen. When they say a word with the long "i" sound, it is preceded by the "aw" sound. Most Mainers will pronounce a word with a long "i" the same way as the rest of the country. Example: The word pride is pronounced "prīd". But many of the Way Down East Mainers pronounce it "praw-īd". It takes some practice to master this way of speaking. But be aware, if this quirk will help you understand what they are talkin' about more quickly, then all the better. It sounds much like Australians say their long "i".

Any word ending in "r", especially "er" or "ar" are replaced by the "uh" sound. It could just as easily be replaced by the "ah" sound. The "r" is rarely pronounced.

In the same way words ending in "er" or "ar" never have the "r" pronounced – the "g" of the "ing" sound is rarely pronounced– only when someone is trying to be very emphatic or trying to emphasize a point.

Often, just plain English is nothing impressive, in itself. BUT add a distinctive regional accent and it becomes a real treasure. Every dialect has been created by a special group of characters. Every dialect creates its own aura. If a person speaks it well, they take on the mystique from which the accent and culture come. Ya know what I mean?

When you consider how many languages have been incorporated into the American English – root words, prefixes, and suffixes – French, Spanish, Greek, and so forth, is it any wonder you find pockets and territories where the language has been customized by the locals to meet their particular needs and reflect their way of life?

Ignatius L Donnelly (mentioned earlier in the Introduction) was a lawyer, farmer, writer, pseudo historian, amateur scientist, and primarily known for his theories on the history of Atlantis and Shakespearian authorship. He determined that "similarity of spelling does not indicate similarity of either pronunciation or meaning."

Just in the US, alone, there are numerous pockets of dialects. How fortunate we are to have such a wide variety – such treats! Not to mention our own dear Canadian neighbors with a number of dialects and languages of their own. And who wouldn't be entertained by the happy, romantic tones that our warm-hearted Mexican/American neighbors have. What a shame it would be to lose the distinctive and entertaining variety we have to enjoy – and all fairly close at hand.

Please, sit back and enjoy this one aspect of our country's unique, playful way of communicating – The Wicked Official Maine way.

Pronunciation Key

    The following letters, symbols, and combination of letters have been custom made and will help you out with translatin' your regular English language into the distinctive and downright comfy way of talkin' like a Mainah.

Dictionary Key

Vowels

Letters & Symbols	Sound Examples	Notes
A, a	crab, math	
ā	tape, whale	
ah	path, hearth	
aw	gone, ball, caught	
E, e	enter, sent	
ē	free, leave	
I, i	knit, bit	
ī	tide, pride	Often in the Way Down East (WDE) pronunciation of the long "ī", the "aw" sound precedes the "i" sound. The word pride would be pronounced praw-īd, much as an Australian would say it.
ing	calling, doing	In Maine, any word ending in "ing" is usually pronounced without the "g". You may hear the "g" pronounced at times when it is needed for emphasis or to help make a point. The "g" is not dropped when it is part of the body of a word, such as bring or fling.
O, o	pot, rot	
ō	hope, dope	

o͞o	cool, dupe	Same as "ū".
oo	hook, look	
ou	cloud, shroud	"ou" may also carry the dull sounds of "ou" as in could or should.
ow	cow, flower	In rare instances, it carries the long "o", as in owe.
U, u	stud, huff	
ū	blue, coup	Same as "o͞o".
u	put, foot	Some people say r"u"f, instead of ro͞of.
uh	power, would be *Pronounced pow-uh or pow-ah.*	When a word ends in "er", "ar", "or", "ur", or "ir", they take on the "uh" sound in Maine. Also, the "uh" and "ah" sound are interchangeable in these situations.
Y, y	deny, sandy, young, yet, yacht, yank	The "y" can carry the long "i" sound or long "e" sound, or even the "yuh" sound, or "ye", "yo", or "y o͞o" – even the "bē-y o͞o-tuh-ful" sound.

Consonants

Letters	Sound Examples	Notes
B, b	box, lube	
C, c	corn, cat, circle, cinema	This can represent the "k" sound or the "s" sound.
ch	chug, chump	
D, d	dug, done	
F, f	fish, lift	
G, g	gull, glue	"g" may be silent, as in gnat. It may also have the "j" sound, as in digest.
gh	cough, laugh, through, thorough	"g" combined with an "h" forms an "f" sound. It can also be silent, as in though.

J, j	jump, jewelry	The "j" sound may occur where there is a "g", as in digest or gorge.
K, k	kitten, kite	
L, l	lawn, felt	
M, m	mouse, matter	
N, n	nook, soon	
P, p	pony, apart	The "p" can be silent as in the following: ptomaine or pterodactyl – or make the "f" sound when combined with an "h".
ph	phantom, phrase (f)	
Q, q	quest, quota	The "q" most always makes the "k" sound.
R, r	read, rough	In Wicked Official Main language, when the "r" is at the end of a word, it is usually pronounced "uh" or "ah" or dropped, altogether. Examples: water = wah-tuh coward = cow-ud whisper = wis-puh
S, s	sudden, south	The "s" may also carry the "z" sound, as in suds, clothes, or the "zh" sound you hear in beige, pleasure, or measure.
sc	scatter (sk), sceptic, scepter, scenery	"sc" usually makes the "sk" sound, as in scant or scout. Or the "c" may be silent, as in scent or scenic.
sch	scholar (sk), schlep (sh)	These letters, sch, form the "sk" sound, as in school and schedule. It can also make the "sh" sound, as in schnapps and schmaltz.
T, t	turf, tent	The "t" may also carry the "ch" sound, as in mature and fortune.
Th "th"	thin, myth, father, heather	"th" may carry another sound, as in mother and feather.
tion	ambition	This "t" family sound is pronounced "shun", as in notion and motion.
V, v	vote, dove	

W, w	want, wet	The "w" is silent when followed by "r", like write and wrong.
wh	while, whether	The "wh" sound may involve a slight huffing sound or be silent, as in whip. Also, the "h" may dominate the duo in cases such as who or whole.
X, x	fix, mixture	These "x" words carry the "iks" sound, but may carry the "z" sound, as in <u>X</u>ylophone or <u>X</u>erox. The letter "x" is pronounced "ecks" and can be seen in the word <u>X</u>-ray.
Y, y	folly, why, synagogue	There are a number of sounds associated with a "y". It can be a silent "y" (pra<u>y</u>er), long "ē" (foll<u>y</u>), a short "i" (s<u>y</u>mpathy), or a unique sound, as in <u>y</u>esterday and <u>y</u>atter. It can also sound like a long "ī" (why). Note: The word "you" is very likely to be pronounced as "yuh" or "ya" UNLESS you are trying to make point.
Z, z	zest, doze, zombie	
"zh"		This stands for the sound you get in words like beige or plea<u>s</u>ure.

First letter of the English Alphabet A,a (ā)

Word	Pronunciation Examples	Notes
ā	cape, April	
a	had, map	
a	class, pass	This "a" is pronounced "ah" in these words.
a	abrupt, appear	This "a" is pronounced "uh".
AA	Alcoholics Uh-nonimus	This "a" is pronounced "uh". Alcoholics starts with a short "a" and Anonymous starts with the "uh" sound.
aardvark	ahd-vahk	Starts with the "ah" sound and ends in "ahk" (drop the "r").
Aaron	Āuh-run	Moses' brother.
ABA	Uh-mār-ruh-kun Bah Uh-sō-s-ē-ā-shun	American Bar Association.
abalone	ab-uh-lō-nē	
abbot	ab-ut	
Abel	Ā-bul	Second son of Adam and Eve – was killed by his brother, Cain.
abhor	1) ab-hōah 2) ab-hōuh	
abhorrent	ab-haw-runt	
abide	uh-bīd	
abjure	1) ab-jōor 2) ab-jōo-uh	
abnormal	ab-naw-mul	No "r" sound.
abnormality	ab-naw-mal-uh-tē	
aboard	uh-bō-ud	

aborning	uh-bawn-in	
abort	uh-bō-ut	
abortion	1) uh-bōer-shun 2) uh-bō-uh-shun 3) uh-baw-shun *used most often.	
abortive	uh-bot-iv	
about	1) uh-bout 2) 'bout	Often, the "a" is dropped, as in "bout time you got hē-uh".
about face	1) uh-bout fāc 2) 'bout fāc	
above board	uh-buv bō-ud	
abscond	ub-skawnd	
absent minded	ab-sunt mīn-did	WDE: ab-sunt-mawīn-did
absorb	ub-sawb	
absorbent	ub-saw-bunt	
absorption	ub-sawp-shun	
abutment	uh-but-munt	
accelerator	ek-sel-uh-rāt-uh	
accord	1) uh-kawd 2) uh-kō-ud	
accordance	uh-kawd-uns	
according	uh-kawd-in'	Oftentimes, the "g" is dropped. "uh-kawd-in'"
accordingly	uh-kawd-in-lē	
accordion	uh-kaud-ē-un	
accounting	uh-kount-in'	
accounter	uh-kōot-uh	To provide clothing or equipment.

accounterments
  or accoutrements
	uh-kōōt-uh-munts
	  uh-kōōt-ruh-munts	

acculturate	uh-kul-chuh-rit	
acetone	a-suh-tōn	
acetylene	uh-set-uh-lēn	
achievement	uh-chēv-munt	
acidify	uh-sid-uh-fī	WDE: uh-sid-uh-faw-ī
acorn	ā-kawn	
acquire	uh-kwī-uh	
acre	ā-kuh	
acreage	1) āk-rij 2) āk-uh-rij	
across the board	uh-kros thuh bōud	
acrylic	uh-kril-ik	
acting	ak-tin'	The "g" is dropped.
actor	ak-tuh	
acupuncture	ak-yū-punk-chuh	
adder	ad-uh	
addict	1) ad-ikt 2) uh-dikt-ed	
adhere	ad-hē-uh	
adjourn	1) ud-jurn 2) uh-jurn*	*Used most of the time.
administration	ad-min-uh-strā–shun	
admire	ad-mī-uh	
admired	ad-mī-ud	
adore	uh-dō-uh	

adorn	uh-dawn	
adultery	1) uh-dul-tuh-rē 2) uh-dul-trē	Adultery is not really accepted but is fairly well-tolerated, usually. There is also a considerable number of folks just plain livin' together who have children. Ya never know whose last name they might take.
adventurer	ad-vench-uh-ruh	
adversarial	ad-vuh-sār-ē-ul	In the past, there were some adversarial (or hostile) feelings between the locals and people from away. Fortunately, these days, those feelings have lessened.
adversary	ad-vuh-sār-ē	
advertise	ad-vuh-tīz	
advertisement	ad vuh-tīz-munt	
advertorial	ad-vuh-taw-rē-ul	
advisory	ad-vīz-uh-rē	
aerie	ā-uh-rē	The high nest of a bird of prey. There was an interesting study goin' on in Acadia National Park where they were keeping count of the number of Peregrine Falcons and their offspring, as well as the locations of their nests, their aerie.
afar	uh-fah	
affair	uh-fā-uh	
afferent	af-uh-rent	
afford	uh-fō-ud	
afire	uh-fī-uh	
AFL CIO	Uh-mār-i-kun Fed-uh-rā-shun ov Lā-buh and Kon-gres ov In-dust-rē -ul Ogon-īz-ā-shun	American Federation of Labor and Congress of Industrial Organization.
a-flutter	uh-flut-uh	

aforementioned	uh-fō-uh-men-chund	
afore said	uh-fō-uh sed	
afore thought	uh-fō-uh thot	
aft	ah-ft	<u>Not</u> aft.
after	ahf-tuh	
after birth	ahf-tuh berth	
after burner	ahf-tuh burn-uh	
afterward	1) aftuh-wud 2) aftuh-wood	
again	uh-gin	
agar	ag-ah	
ageratum	ag-uh-rat-um	
agglomerate	uh-glom-uh-rit	
aglitter	uh-glit-uh	
agriculture	ag-ri-kul-chuh	
ail	ā-ul	
air	ā-uh	
air bag	ā-uh bag	
air base	ā-uh bās	
air borne	ā-uh bawn	
air conditioner	ā-uh kun-dish-un-uh	
air craft	ā-uh krahft	<u>Not</u> kraft.
air craft carrier	ā-uh krahft kār-ē-uh	
Airedale	Āuh-dāul	A large terrier with a wiry coat name after Airedale Valley, in England.
air faire	ā-uh fā-uh	

air field	ā-uh fē-uld	
air force	ā-uh fō-us	
air guitar	1) ā-uh gi-tah 2) ā-uh guh-tah	
air liner	ā-uh līn-uh	
air port	ā-uh pō-ut	
air power	ā-uh pow-uh	
air pressure	ā-uh presh-uh	
air rifle	ā-uh rīf-ul	
air strike	ā-uh strīk	
air tight	ā-uh tīt	
air time	ā-uh tīm	WDE: ā-uh tawīm
airy	ā-uh-rē	
alabaster	aluh-bas-tuh	
a la carte	ah lah kaht	
alar	a-luh	Relating to wings.
Allagash	Al-uh-gash	A wooded wilderness reserve in northern Maine. It has a 92-mile ribbon of lakes, streams, and rivers, surrounded by mountains and lush forests, full of moose, bobcats, eagles, bear, and deer. The Allagash waterfall has a 44ft drop.
alarm	uh-lahm	
alarming	uh-lahm-in'	
alas	ah-lahs	
Alaska	Uh-lahsk-uh	
albacore	al-buh-kō-uh	
albatross	al-buh-tros	

albino	al-bīn-ō	
album	1) al-bum 2) awl-bum	
alder	awl-duh	
ale	ā-ul	
alewife	ā-ul-wīf	A NW Atlantic fish resembling the herring.
Alexander the Great	Al-ex-an-duh thuh Grāt	
Algiers	Al-jē-uz	Capital of Algeria
alibi	al-uh-bī	WDE: al-uh-bawī
alimentary	āl-uh-mentrē	
align	uh-līn	WDE: uh-lawīn
allergen	al-uh-jen	
allergist	al-uh-jist	
allergy	al-uh-jē	
all clear	awl klē-uh	
all fried	awl frīd	WDE: awl frawīd
alliance	uh-lī-uns	
allied	1) al-īd 2) uh-līd	
alligator	al-uh-gā-tuh	
alligator pear	al-uh-gā-tuh pā-uh	
all important	1) awl im-paw-tunt 2) awl im-pō-uh-tunt	
alliteration	alit-uh-rā-shun	
all over	awl ō-vuh	
all night	awl nīt	WDE: awl nawīt

all spice	awl spīs	WDE: awl spawīs
all star	awl stah	
all time	awl tīm	WDE: awl tawīm
allure	uh-lōō-uh	
ally	al-ī	WDE: al-awī
alma mator	1) awl-muh mah-tuh 2) al-muh mah-tuh	
alms	1) ah-mz 2) aw-mz	
along shore	uh-long shō-uh	
along side	uh-long sīd	WDE: uh-long sawīd
alpha particle	al-fuh pah-tik-ul	
alpine	al-pīn	WDE: al-pawīn
alright	awl-rīt	WDE: awl-rawīt
altar	awl-tuh	
altercation	awl-tuh-kā-shun	
alter ego	awl-tuh ēgō	
alternate	1) awl-tuh nāt 2) awl-tuh-nit	
altimeter	al-tim-uh-tuh	
altogether	awl-tōō-ge-"th"-uh	
Alzheimer's	1) Alz-īm-uz 2) Awlz-īm-uz	
amateur	am-uh-chōō-uh	
ambassador	1) am-bas-uh-dō-uh 2) am-bas-uh-duh	
amber	am-buh	

amen	1) ā-men 2) ah-men	
Amerasion	Am-uh-rā-"zh"-un	One of the few words that Mainers pronounce the "r" and say American like other fellow Americans – but some may say Am-uh-rā-"zh"-un.
America	Uh-mār-ik-uh	
American	Uh-mār-uh-kun	
Amerindian	Am-uh-in-dē-un	
ammeter	am-eh-tuh	
amoral	ā-maw-rul	
amorous	am-uh-rus	
amour	uh-mōō-uh	
amorphous	am-aw-fus	
amortize	uh-maw-tīz	
amperage	1) amp-uh-rij 2) amp-rij	
ampere	am-pē-uh	
ampersand	am-puh-sand	A sign meaning *and* (&).
amphitheater	am-fuh-thē-et-uh	
amplifier	amp-luh-fī-uh	
Amsterdam	Am-stuh-dam	Capital of the Netherlands.
amusement park	uh-mūz-munt pahk	
anaerobic	an-uh-rō-bik	
anarchism	an-ahk-izm	
anarchy	an-ah-kē	
ancestor	an-ses-tuh	

anchor	ank-uh	
anchorage	ank-uh-rij	
anchorman	1) ank-uh-man 2) ank-uh-mun	

Andersen, Hans
  Christian
	An-duh-sun, Hahns
	  Krish-chen
		Writer of fairy tales.

andiron	and-ī-on	
and/or	and/aw	
Androscoggin	An-drō-skog-in	A county in Maine.
anemometer	an-uh-mom-eh-tuh	Wind gauge.
anemone	an-em-un-ē	Also the name of a cave in Acadia National Park where these creatures thrive.
aneroid barometer	an-uh-roid buh-rom-uh-tuh	
anger	ang-uh	
angular	ang-you-luh	
Ankara	Ank-uh-ruh	Capital of Turkey.
Ann Arbor	An Ah-buh	City in Michigan.
anniversary	an-uh-ver-suh-rē	
announcer	uh-nown-suh	
annular	an-you-luh	
another	uh-nu-"th"-uh	
Answer	an-suh	
answering machine	an-suh-rin muh-shēn	
Antarctic	Ant-ahk-tik	
Antarctica	Ant-ahk-tik-uh	
ant bear	ant bā-uh	

Wicked Official Maine Dictionary

ant eater	ant ēt-uh	
antechamber	antē-chām-buh	
anterior	antēr-ē-uh	
anther	an-thuh	
anthropomorphism	an-thrō-puh-maw-fizum	
anti	1) ant-ī 2) ant-ē	WDE: ant-awī
anti-aircraft	antē-ā-uh-krahft	
antimacassar	antē-muh-kas-uh	A small cover put on the back or arms of a chair or sofa to protect the furniture from soiling.
antimatter	antē-mat-uh	
antiserum	1) antē-serum 2) anti-serum	
antislavery	1) antē-slāv-rē 2) antī-slāv-rē	
antler	ant-luh	
antsy	ant-sē	Restless, anxious, jittery – so comes the saying, "ants in your pants."
any	1) en-ē 2) in-ē	
anybody	1) en-ē-bud-ē 2) en-ē-baud-ē	
anymore	en-ē-mō-uh	
anytime	en-ē-tīm	WDE: enē-tawīm
anywhere	en-ē-wā-uh	
aorta	ā-aw-tuh	
Apart	uh-paht	
apartheid	uh-pah-tīd	

apartment	1) uh-paht-munt 2) uh-paht-ment	
aperture	1) ap-uh-chōō-uh 2) ap-uh-chur	
aphorism	1) af-aw-izm 2) af-aw-rizm	
apiary	āp-ē-ār-ē	
apparently	'par-ent-lē	Most of the time, a Mainer drops the "a" and simply says 'parently.
appear	uh-pē-uh	
appertain	ap-uh-tān	
appetizer	apuh-tīz-uh	
apple butter	apul-but-uh	
apple pie	apul pī	WDE: apul pawī
applicator	ap-luh-kā-tuh	
applied	uh-plīd	WDE: uh-plawīd
apply	uh-plī	
apportion	uh-pō-uh-shun	
apprise or apprize	uh-prīz	WDE: uh-prawīz
APR	An-yōō-ul Puh-sent-ij Rāt	Annual Percentage Rate
Aqua	ah-kwah	
aquamarine	ahk-wuh-muh-rēn	
aquanaut	ahk-wuh-not	
aqueous humor	ak-wē-us hyōō-muh	
aquiline	1) ak-wi-līn 2) ahk-wuh-lin	
Arabic numerals	Ār-uh-bik nōōm-uh-rulz	1, 2, 3, 4, 5, 6, 7, 8, 9, 0

arable	ār-uh-bul
arachnid	ah-rak-nid
arbiter	ah-bi-tuh
arbitrage	ah-bi-trij
arbitrate	ah-buh-trāt
arbitrator	ah-buh-trā-tuh
arbor	ah-buh
arboreal	uh-bor-ē-ul
arboretum	ah-buh-retum
arborvitae	ah-buh-vit-ē
arc	ahk
arcade	ah-kād
arcane	ah-kān
arch	ahch
archaeology	ahk-ē-oluh-jē
archaic	ah-kā-ik
archangel	ahk-ānjul
archbishop	1) ahk-bishup 2) ahch-bish-up
archdeacon	1) ahk-dēkun 2) ahch-dē-kun
archdiocese	1) ahch-dī-uh-sis 2) ahch-dī-uh-sēz
archduke	ahch-dōōk
archenemy	1) ahch-enemē 2) ahk-enemē
archer	ahch-uh

archetype	ah-kuh-tīp
archiepiscopal	ah-kē-pis-kuh-pul
Archimedes	Ahk-uh-mē-dēz
archipelago	ahk-uh-pel-uh-gō
architect	ahk-uh-tekt
architectonics	ahk-ē-tek-ton-iks
architecture	1) ahk-i-tekt-chuh 2) ahk-uh-tek-chuh
architrave	ahk-i-trāv
archive	ah-kīv
archway	ahch-wā
archy	ah-kē
Arctic	Ahk-tik
Arctic Circle	Ahk-tik Ser-kul
Arctic Ocean	Ahk-tic Ō-shun
ardent	1) ah-dent 2) ah-dunt
ardor	ah-duh
arduous	ahd-yū-us
are	Ah
aren't	ahnt
argent	ah-jent
Argonaut	Ah-gō-not
argosy	ah-guh-sē
Argo	Ah-gō
argue	ahg-yū

argument	ahg-yū-ment	
argumentation	ahg-yū-men-tā-shun	
argumentative	ahg-yū-men-tuh-tiv	
argyle	1) ah-gīl 2) ah-gī-ul	
ark	ahk	
Arkansas	1) Ahk-un-saw 2) Ahk-in-saw	State in the USA. (AR) Capital: Little Rock.
Arc of the Covenant	1) Ahk ov thuh Kuv-i-nent 2) Ahk ov thuh Kuv-uh-nunt	
Arlington	Ah-ling-tun	
arm	ahm	
armada	ah-mah-duh	
armadillo	ahm-uh-dilō	
Armageddon	Ahm-uh-ged-un	
armament	ahm-uh-ment	
armature	ahm-uh-chōōuh	
arm chair	ahm chā-uh	
armed forces	1) ahmd fō-us-ez 2) ahmd faus-ez	Army, Navy, Marines, Air Force, Coast Guard.
Armenia	Ah-mē-nē-uh	West Asian country.
armful	ahm ful	
arm hole	ahm hōl	
armistice	ahm-ist-us	
Armistice Day	Arm-ist-us Dā	Nov. 11th, the anniversary of the armistice of WWI
armlet	ahm-let	

armload	ahm-lōd
armored car	ah-mud kah
armorial	Ah-maur-ē-ul
armor plate	ahm-uh plāt
armory	ahm-uh-rē
arm pit	ahm pit
arm rest	ahm rest
army	ah-mē
Arnold Benedict	Ah-nuld Benuh-dikt
Aroostook	Uh-rōōs-tick
arpeggio	ah-pej-ēō
arrears	uh-rē-uz
arsenal	1) ah-sen-ul 2) ah-sun-ul
arsenic	ahs-nik
arson	ah-sun
art	aht
art deco	aht dekō
arterial	ah-tēr-ē-ul
Arteriole	ah-tēr-ē-ōl
arteriosclerosis	ah-tēr-ē-ō-skluh-rō-sis
artery	ah-tuh-rē
artesian well	ah-tē-"zh"-un wel
art film	aht film
artful	aht-ful

art house	aht hows	
arthritis	ahth-rī-tis	
arthro	ahth-rō	
arthroscope	ahth-rō-skōp	21st President of the USA
Arthur, Chester Alan	Ah-thuh, Chest-uh Alun	
artichoke	ah-tuh-chōk	
article	ah-ti-kul	
articulator	ah-tik-yōō-lāt-uh	
artifact	ah-ti-fakt	
artifice	ah-ti-fīs	
artificial	ah-ti-fīsh-ul	
artillery	ah-til-uh-rē	
artisan	ah-tuh-sun	
artist	ah-tist	
artistic	ah-tis-tik	
artistry	ah-tis-trē	
artless	aht-les	
Arts and Crafts	Ahts and Crahfs	
ascorbic acid	uh-skaw-bik asid	
ascribe	uh-skrīb	
ashore	uh-shō-uh	
Asia Minor	Ā-"zh"-uh Mīn-uh	
aside	uh-sīd	
asinine	1) ah-sin-īn 2) as-in-īn	Stupid, ridiculous behavior (also known as an asshole).

ask	ahsk
askance	ahsk-uns
asking price	ahskin' prīs
aspirator	as-puh-rā-tuh
aspire	uh-spī-uh
ass	ahs
ass hole (slang)	ahs-hōl

1) Body part known as the anus.
2) Personality more abrasive than a jerk.
3) Can be an adjective describing a person whose personality is very unpleasant; callous.

assign	uh-sīn
assure	ah-shōō-uh
astride	ah-strīd WDE: uh-strawīd
asunder	ah-sun-duh
athlete	1) ath-uh-lēt 2) ath-lēt
athwart	uh-thwot
atmosphere	at-mus-fē-uh
atomic energy	uh-tom-ik en-uh-jē
atomic number	uh-tom-ik num-buh
atomizer	atom-īz-uh
attainder	uh-tān-duh
attire	uh-tī-uh
atwitter	uh-twit-uh
auburn	aw-bun
audiometer	1) aw-dē-o-met-uh 2) awd-ē-om-i-tuh

47

auger	awg-uh	
augur	aw-guh	
augury	awg-yōō-rē	
Augusta	Uh-gust-uh	Capital of Maine.
aunt	1) ahnt 2) awnt	
austere	aws-tē-uh	
author	aw-thuh	
authorship	aw-thuh-ship	
autograph	aw-tō-grahf	
avail	uh-vā-ul	
avatar	av-uh-tah	
avocado	ah-vuh-kah-dō	
award	uh-wod	
aware	uh-wā-uh	
awkward	awk-wud	
awry	uh-rī	WDE: uh-rawī
Axminister	Ax-min-uh-stuh	The town in England where this type of carpet was first made.
Ayah	1) Ā-uh 2) Ā-ah	Yes, or I agree.
aye	ī	Yes, or affirmative vote.
Azores	Āzō-uz	

Second letter of the English Alphabet B,b (bē)

Word	Pronunciation Examples	Notes
baby	bā-bē	
baby boomer	bā-bē bōō-muh	
baby sitter	bā-bē sit-uh	
bachelor	1) bach-luh 2) bach-uh-luh	
Bachelor of Arts	Bach-luh of Ahts	
bachelor's button	bach-luz but-un	
back biter	bak bīt-uh	Someone who talks negatively about someone else when they're not present.
back board	bak bō-ud	
back breaking	bak br-āk-in'	
backer	bak-uh	
backfire	bak fī-uh	
backing	bak-in'	Reminder: Mainers usually drop the g of "ing", unless it is needed for emphasis.
back order	bak aw-duh	
back side	bak sīd	WDE: bak sawīd
back slapper	bak slap-uh	
back slide	bak slīd	
back stair	bak stā-uh	WDE: bak slawīd
back stairs	bak stā-uz	
backward	bak-wud	
backwater	bak-wot-uh	

back woods	bak woodz	A sparsely populated area. It may or may not be heavily wooded. It's the same as living in the "boonies."
badger	ba-juh	
bad tempered	bad tem-pud	
Baedeker	Bā-duh-kuh	
bag piper	bag pīp-uh	
bail	bā-ul	
baked	bā-kt	1) Food cooked in the oven. 2) (slang) Heavily under the influence of alcohol or some other recreational drug, as in being "toasted".
baker	bāk-uh	
baker's dozen	bāk-uz duzun	
bakery	bāk-rē	
baking powder	bāk-in pow-duh	
balderdash	bawl-duh-dash	Nonsense.
bale	1) bāl 2) bā-ul	
balk	bawk	
ballad	bal-ud	
ball bearing	1) bawl bār-in 2) bawl bār-un	
ballistic (slang)	buh-list-ik	Out of control, usually because of severe anger or rage – "They went ballistic."
ballpeen hammer	1) bol-pēn ham-uh 2) bawl-pēn ham-uh	
ball player	bawl plā-uh	
balmy	1) baw-mē 2) bah-mē	

bandoleer	band-ō-lē-ah	
Bangor	Bang-aw	City in eastern/central Maine.
banister	ban-is-tuh	
bank card	bank kahd	
baker	bā-kuh	
baking	bā-kin'	
banner	ban-uh	
banter	ban-tuh	
bar	bah	
barb	bahb	
barbaric	bah-bār-ik	
barbarism	bah-buh-rizm	
barbarize	bah-buh-rīz	
barbarous	bah-buh-rus	
barbecue	bah-buh-kyōō	
barbed wire	bahb'd wī-uh	
barbel	bah-bul	Thread-like growth from the lips or jaws of certain fish.
barbell	bah-bel	
barber	bah-buh	
barberry	bah-be-rē	
barbiturate	bah-bich-uh-rit	
barb wire	bahb wī-uh	
barcarolle	bah-kuh-rōl	
Barcelona	Bah-suh-lōn-uh	

bar code	bah kōd	
bard	bahd	
bare	bā-uh	
bare back	bā-uh bak	
bare bones	bā-uh bōnz	
bare faced	bā-uh fā-sd	
bare foot	bā-uh foot	
bare handed	bā-uh handed	
bare headed	bā-uh hed-id	
bare legged	bā-uh leg-ed	
barely	bā-uh-lē	
bargain	bah-gin	
bargain counter	bah-gin kown-tuh	
barge	bahj	
bar graph	bah grahf	Never pronounced "graf".
Bar Harbor	Bah Hah-buh	A resort town on beautiful Mount Desert Island, just off the coast of down east Maine.
baritone	1) bār-uh-tōn 2) bār-i-tōn	
barium	bār-ē-um	
bark	bahk	1) Outside covering of a tree. 2) Sound a dog makes. 3) To speak sharply. 4) A sailing boat. 5) To bark up the wrong tree.
bar keeper	bah kēp-uh	
barker	bah-kuh	One who talks loudly to get people's attention.

barley	bah-lē	
bar maid	bah mād	
bar mitzvah	bah mitz-vuh	A ceremony for a Jewish girl of 13 years of age to celebrate coming of age.
barn	bahn	
barnacle	bahn-uh-kul	
barn burner	bahn burn-uh	
barn storm	bahn stawm	
barn yard	bahn yahd	
barometer	buh-rom-uh-tuh	
baron	bār-un	
barrage	buh-rah-"zh"	
barred	bahd	
barrier	bār-ē-uh	
barrister	bār-ist-uh	
bar room	bah room	
bar tender	bah tend-uh	
barter	bah tuh	
base board	bās bō-ud	
base runner	bās run-uh	
basket	1) bahs-ket 2) bahs-kit	
basket ball	bahs-ket bawl	
basket weave	bahs-ket wēv	
bass	bahs	Rarely hear bās or bas.

Bass Harbor	Bahs Hah-buh	A Coastal town on the SW side of Mount Desert Island.
basso	1) basō 2) bah-sō	
bastard	bah-stud	Dictionary Definition: 1) An illegitimate child of illegitimate birth. 2) Inferior, sham. In Maine, it is not uncommon to have a child by one parent. It is NOT looked down upon. Also, bastard is used at times as a greeting, such as, "Well, hullo! You old bahstud, you!" There is no offense meant and none taken. Of course, it can be used in a negative way, too. So, calling someone a bahstud in anger, especially, is <u>not</u> a nice thing.
bat (old bat)	No change.	1) A stout club, as one used in baseball, etc. 2) A small, nocturnal, flying animal (furry, too). 3) Not to bat an eye: not to be surprised, nor show it. 4) If someone is called an old bat, it is meant as derogatory. It implies the person is an ugly (looking and personality) woman. Usually known to be <u>not</u> nice.
bath	bahth	You rarely hear a Mainer say <u>bath</u>. It's usually bahth.
bath house	bahth hows	
bath mat	bahth mat	
bath robe	bahth rōb	
bath tub	bahth tub	
battering ram	bat-uh-rin' ram	
beach comber	bēch kōm-uh	
beach wear	bēch wā-uh	

beagle	bē-gul	The dictionary says this dog is "a small hound with short legs and drooping ears." I must add to this, as a beagle has many more important characteristics that are notable, such as their color. They are white, tan, and black, most often with a black saddle shape over their back. Their sense of smell is very acute, as it is a hunting dog that relies on smell to track their prey. Because a Beagle pup is so cute, many people get one, not knowing what they're in for. That adorable face is not that of a lap dog. He is a hunter and needs lots of exercise and training. By the way, a Beagle doesn't have especially short legs. That sounds more like a Basset Hound.
beaker	bē-kuh	
bear	bā-uh	
beard	bē-ud	
bearing	bār-in'	
bearish	bār-ish	
bear skin	bā-uh skin	
beast	bē-st	1) Large, four-footed animal. 2) One who is gross, brutal, etc... 3) Nickname for a rugged, aggressive sportsperson.
beatify	bē-at-uh-fī	
beautify	byōō-ti-fī	
beauty parlor	byōō-tē pah-luh	
beaver	bē-vuh	
because	bē-kaus	Many times, you'll hear the "be" dropped, and people will just say "kuz".
bedding	bed-in'	
bedraggled	bē-drag-uld	

bedevil	bē-dev-ul	The dictionary says "to plague or bewilder". I must take this a bit further and add that it could be describing a person who is being plagued by a spiritual creature called a demon, multiple demons, or the devil himself. I guess it depends on what you believe.
bedeviled	bē-dev-uld	
bedsore	bed-sō-uh	The dictionary states this sore is "on a bedridden person which is "caused by chafing". However, about 34 years of my being an active RN taught me that a bedsore occurs when flesh doesn't get the circulation of blood and fluids it needs from too much pressure to the area, usually from immobility. The first sign is a reddened area that doesn't go away. If the pressure continues, the skin will die and leave an open sore. This is a "bedsore".
bedtime	bed tīm	
bee hive	bē hīv	
bee keeper	bē kēp-uh	
bee line	bē līn	See the section on "Sayings" in this book for more info on bee line.
beer	bē-uh	
bees wax	bēz wax	
before	bē-fō-uh	
beggar	beg-uh	
beggarly	beg-uh-lē	
beginner	bē-gin-uh	
begrime	bē-grīm	
beguile	bē-gī-ul	
behalf	bē-hahf	
behavior	bē-hāv-yuh	

behind	bē-hīnd	WDE: bē-hawīnd
belabor	bē-lā-buh	
be leaguer	bē lēg-uh	
bebe	bē-bē	
belligerent	buh-lij-uh-runt	
bell jar	bel jah	
bell pepper	bel pep-uh	
Belshazzar	1) Bel-shaz-ah 2) Bel-shaz-uh	In the Bible, the last king of Babylon.
bench mark	bench mahk	
benefactor	ben-uh-fakt-uh	
benign	bē-nīn	
Bermuda shorts	Buh-myōō-duh shawts	
berserk	buh-zerk	
besetting	bē-set-in'	
beside	bē-sīd	WDE: bē-sawīd
besmear	bē-smē-uh	
bespatter	bē-spat-uh	
bestride	bē-strīd	WDE: bē-strawīd
beta blocker	bāt-uh blok-uh	
beta particle	bāt-uh pah-tik-ul	
betide	bē-tīd	WDE: bē-tawīd
better	bet-uh	
betterment	bet-uh-munt	
bettor	bet-uh	

between	buh-twēn	
bevel gear	bevul gē-uh	
beverage	bev-rij	
beware	bē-wā-uh	
bewilder	bē-wil-duh	
Bible	Bī-bul	
bibliography	1) bib-lē-og-ruh-fē 2) bib-lē-og-rah-fē	
bicarbonate of soda	1) bī-kah-bun-āt ov sō-duh 2) bī-kah-buh-nit ov sō-duh	
bicentennial	bī-sen-ten-ē-ul	
bicker	bik-uh	
bicuspid	bī-kus-pid	
bicycle	bī-sik-ul	
bide	bīd	WDE: bawīd
bifocals	bī-fō-kulz	
Big Dipper	Big Dip-uh	
big hearted	big haht-ed	
big horn	big hawn	
bight	bīt	
big time	big tīm	WDE: big tawīm
bilateral	bī-lat-uh-rul	
bile	bī-ul	
bilingual	bī-ling-wul	
bill board	bil bō-ud	
billiards	bil-ē-udz	

billing	bil-in'	
billion	bil-ē-un	
billionaire	bil-ē-un-ā-uh	
bill of fare	bil ov fā-uh	
bimonthly	bī-munth-lē	
binder	bīn-duh	
binding	bind-in'	
binocular	buh-nok-yōō-luh	
biological warfare	bī-ul-oj-ikul waw-fā-uh	
biopsy	bī-op-sē	
bipartisan	bī-paht-is-un	
bipartite	bī-pah-tīt	Involving two.
biped	bī-ped	WDE: bawī-ped
bipolar	bī-pōl-uh	
binds eye	binds ī	WDE: binds awī
Bismarck	Biz-mahk	Capital of North Dakota.
bit	No change.	1) A small amount. 2) Goes in the horse's mouth and attaches to the bridle. 3) Something that curbs or controls. 4) A tool for drilling or boring. 5) A unit of information.
bitter	bit-uh	
bitter sweet	bit-uh swēt	
bizarre	buz-ah	
blabber mouth	blab-uh mow-th	
black board	blak bō-ud	

black mark	blak mahk	
black market	blak mah-ket	
black power	blak pow-uh	
black thorn	blak thawn	
bladder	blad-uh	
blare	blā-uh	
blarney	blah-nē	Someone who is blessed with "the blarney", especially an Irishman, is one who has a very charmin' way about them, even as they may stretch the truth a little while speakin' flatteringly to females. It's all in fun, not meant to be hurtful or insultin' in any way.
The Blarney Stone	Thuh Blah-nē Stōn	The Blarney Stone is in Ireland. It is said that anyone who kisses the Blarney Stone will gain the gift of blarney – this is, the ability to speak with charm and flattery, usually to someone of the opposite sex.
blast	blahst	It's very unlikely you would hear a Mainer say blast.
blast off	blahst off	
blazer	blā-zuh	
blender	blen-duh	
blessed	1) blest 2) bles'd 3) bles'ed	
blight	blīt	
blind	blīnd	WDE: blawīnd
blinders	blīnd-uz	
blinker	blēnk-uh	
blister	blis-tuh	

blistering	blis-tuh-rin'	This refers not to blisters developing so much as referrin' to the atmosphere being very hot or intense.
blizzard	bliz-ud	
block buster	blok bust-uh	
blood pressure	blud presh-uh	
blood sucker	blud suk-uh	
bloomers	blo͞om-uz	
blooming	blo͞om-in'	
blooper	blo͞o-puh	
blotter	blot-uh	
blow dry	blō drī	
blow hard	blō hahd	
blow torch	blō tawch	
blubber	blub-uh	
blue	blo͞o	1) Color of a clear sky. 2) Sad, gloomy. 3) Unexpected – "out of the blue".
blueberry	blo͞o-berē	High production in Maine.
blue collar	blo͞o kol-uh	
blue grass	blo͞o grahs	1) Grass with bluish tint. 2) Fast, bluesy country music.
blue whale	blo͞o wā-ul	Largest animal.
bluing	blo͞o-in'	1) Rinse used on white fabrics to prevent yellowing. 2) A liquid rubbed onto the barrel of a gun to protect the metal.
blunder	blun-duh	
blunder buss	blun-duh bus	

bluster	blus-tuh	
boar	bō-ah	
Board	bō-ud	
boater	bōt-uh	
boating	bōt-in'	
body guard	bawd-ē-gahd	
Boer	Bō-uh	A South African of Dutch descent.
boil	bōē-ul	
boiler	bōē-ul-uh	
bolster	bōls-tuh	
bombard	bom-bahd	
bombardier	bom-buh-dē-uh	
bomber	bom-uh	
Bonaparte, Napoleon	Bon-uh-paht, Nuh-pōl-ē-un	A French military leader and Emperor. (1804-1815).
bond paper	bond pā-puh	
boner (slang)	bōn-uh	1) A blunder of sorts. 2) A male erection.
bonfire	bon-fī-uh	
bonkers (slang)	bon-kuz	Crazy.
book maker	book māk-uh	
book mark	book mahk	
book store	book stō-uh	
boomer	bōōm-uh	
boomerang	bōōm-uh-rang	
boonies	bōōn-ēz	About the same as being out in the boondocks – that is, way out of town.

booster shot	bōōst-uh shot	
bootie (slang)	bōōt-ē	Refers to the buttocks or derriere, such as when one dances, you may shake your bootie.
border	bawd-uh	
border land	bawd-uh land	
border line	bawd-uh līn	
bore	bō-uh	
boredom	1) bō-ud-um 2) bō-uh-dum	
born	bawn	
born again	bawn uh-gin	
Borneo	Baw-nē-ō	
boron	1) bōr-on 2) bawr-on	
borough	bur-ō	A self-governing incorporated town.
borrow	baw-rō	
borzoi	baw-zōē	
Boston	Baw-stun	Seaport and capital of MA (Massachusetts). They have a distinct accent – sort of a cousin to Maine's. They are a wonderful, proud, brave, loveable, STRONG people.
bother	baw-"th"-uh	
boudoir	bōōd-wah	
boulder	bōl-duh	
boulevard	1) bōō-luh-vahd 2) buhl-uh vahd	
bouncer	bowns-uh	

bounder	bown-duh	A cad.
boutonniere	bōō-tun-ē-uh	
bower	bow-uh	
boulder	bōl-duh	
box car	box kah	
boxer	box-uh	
boxing	boxin'	
boy friend	1) bōē-frend 2) boi-frend	
braggart	brag-ut	
brain storm	brān stawm	
brass tacks	brahs taks	Not pronounced bras.
bread winner	bred win-uh	
breaker	brāk-uh	
break water	brāk waw-tuh	
breather	brē-"th"-uh	
breeding	brē-din'	
brewery	brōō-uh-rē	
briar	brī-uh	
bribe	brīb	
bric a brac	brik brak	Nick nacks or ornaments. The middle "a" usually isn't said.
brick layer	brik lā-uh	
brick laying	brik lā-in'	
bride	brīd	WDE: brawīd
bride groom	brīd groom	

Bridgeport	Brij-pō-ut	A seaport in the state of Connecticut.
bridle	brīd-ul	
bridle path	brīd-ul pahth	Not p<u>a</u>th.
brier	brī-uh	
brigadier general	brig-uh-dē-uh gen-rul	
bright	brīt	
brine	brīn	
broad	brawd	1) Wide. 2) Slang for a female, NOT very respectful.
broad side	brawd sīd	WED: brawd sawīd
broad sword	brawd sō-ud	
brochure	1) brō-shōō-uh 2) brō-shō-uh	
broiler	brōē-ul-uh	
broker	brōk-uh	
brokerage	brōk-uh-rij	
bromide	brō-mīd	WDE: bro-mawīd
broncobuster	bronco-bust-uh	
Bronx	Brawnks	Borough of New York City. They have a hardy, earthy accent. Congratulations and best wishes in keepin' it.
brooder	brōōd-uh	
brood mare	brōōd mā-uh	
Brooklyn	Brook-lin	Borough of New York City. These folks also have a distinctive, great, and light-hearted accent. Best wishes to you keepin' it.
brother	bru-"th"-uh	

brown sugar	brown shug-uh	
browser	browz-uh	
bruiser	brōōz-uh	
buccaneer	buk-un-ē-uh	
buck board	buk bō-ud	
buckler	buk-luh	
buck passer	buk pahs-uh	
buffer	buf-uh	
bug bear	bug bā-uh	
bug eyed	bug īd	WDE: bug awīd
bugger (slang)	bug-uh	While this word is not found in a normal dictionary, it is a word of double meaning. 1) A difficult challenge – as when tryin' to change a tire, the lug nuts are stuck – "That's a real bugger." 2) Can be used to describe a small or adorable child – "He's a cute little bugger."
bull dozer	bul dōz-uh	
bulletin board	bul-uh-tun bō-ud	
bull horn	bul hawn	
bummer (slang)	bum-uh	An experience that is always unpleasant, a downer, or sad.
bumper	bump-uh	
bumper sticker	bump-uh stik-uh	I saw one around town that read: "Abortion: one dead, one wounded" – impressive.
bumptious	bump-shus	It means to be disagreeably conceited.
bungee cord	bunjē kawd	
Bunsen burner	Bun-sun burn-uh	

bunting	bun-tin'	
burdock	bur-dok	This usually refers to a plant with prickly, purple-flowered heads. But it can also refer to a person who is annoyin' or irritatin' and often hard to get rid of!
burgher	ber-guh	Citizen of a town.
burglar	burg-luh	
burgomaster	1) burgō mahst-uh 2) burgō mast-uh	
business card	biz-nes kahd	
butcher	buch-uh	
butler	but-luh	
butter	but-uh	
butter fingers	but-uh fing-uz	
buy	bī	WDE: bawī
buyer	bī-uh	
buzzard	buz-ud	
by pass	1) bī pahs 2) bī pas (rarely)	
by stander	bī stand-uh	

Third letter of the English Alphabet C,c (sē)

Word	Pronunciation Examples	Notes
cabernet	kab-uh-nā	
cabinet	kab-net	The "in" part is often left out.
cabinet maker	kab-net māk-uh	
cabin fever	kab-in fē-vuh	
cable car	kā-bul kah	
café	kaf-ā	
cager	kāj-uh	A basketball player.
cagey or cagy	kā-jē	
cairn	1) kahrn 2) kern	A conical heap of stones, in Scotland, especially, built as a monument.
Caesar	Sēz-uh	Any emperor or dictator, but especially the title of the Roman emperors from 27 BC to AD 138.
calamari	kal-uh-mah-rē	Squid cooked as food.
calcium carbonate	cal-sē-um kah-bun-āt	
calculator	kal-kyōō-lā-tuh	
caldera	kawl-duh-ruh	
caldron	kawl-drun	
calendar	1) kal-en-duh 2) kal-un-duh	
calf	kahf	
calves	kahvz	
caliber	1) kal-i-buh 2) kal-uh-buh	

California	Kal-i-fawn-ē-uh	State in the SW United States on the Pacific Coast. (CA) Capital: Sacramento.
caliper	1) kal-uh-puh 2) kal-i-puh	
call forwarding	kawl faw-wud-in	
calligraphy	kal-ig-ruh-fē	
calling	kawl-in'	
calling card	kawlin' kahd	
calm	kahm	
calumniate	kah-lum-nē-āt	
calumny	kal-um-nē	Slander.
Calvary	Kal-vuh-rē	The place where Jesus was crucified.
camaraderie	kum-rahd-uh-rē	
camcorder	kam-kawd-uh	
camera	kam-ruh	
camera man	1) kam-ruh man 2) kam-ruh mun	
chamomile	1) kam-ō-mē-ul 2) kam-uh-mī-ul	
campanile	kam-puh-nē-lē	
camper	kamp-uh	
camp fire	kamp fī-uh	
camphor	kam-fuh	
cam shaft	kam shahft	
Canada	Kan-uh-duh	Country north of the US (our neighbors), just full of great ways of talkin'.
canard	kun-ahd	

cancer	kan-suh
candor	1) kan-duh 2) kan-daw
canine	kā-nīn
canister	kan-is-tuh
canker	kank-uh
cantata	1) kan-ta-tuh 2) kun-tah-tuh
canter	kan-tuh
cantor	kan-tah
canvass	kan-vus
caper	kā-puh
capital letter	kap-uh-tul let-uh
caplet	kap-let
Capricorn	Kap-ruh-kawn
captor	kap-tuh
car	kah
Caracas	1) Kah-rak-us 2) Kah-rahk-us
caracul	kah-ruh-kul
carafe	kah-rahf
caramel	1) kah-ra-mel 2) kah-mul 3) kar-uh-mul
caramelize	1) kar-uh-mul-īz 2) kahr-mul-īz
carapace	kār-uh-pus
car bide	kah bīd

carbohydrate	kah-bō-hī-drāt
carbonic acid	kah-bonic asid
carbon	kah-bun
carbon dioxide	kah-bun dī-ox-īd
carbon paper	kah-bun pā-puh
carcass	kah-kus
carcinogen	kah-sin-uh-jin
car coat	kah kōt
card	kahd
cardboard	kahd-bō-ud
cardiograph	kahd-ē-ō-grahf
cardiovascular	kahd-ē-ō-vas-kyōō-luh
cards	kahdz
card sharp	kahd shahp

Also known as a card shark – kahd shahk.

care	kā-uh
care free	kā-uh frē
care giver	kā-uh giv-uh
care worn	kā-uh wawn
car fare	kah fā-uh
car jacking	kah jak-in'
carnivore	1) kah-nuh-vō-uh 2) kah-ni-vō-uh
carp	kahp
car pool	kah pōōl
car port	kah pō-ut

carrot	kār-ut	
carry over	kārē ōv-uh	
Carson City	Kah-sun Sit-ē	Capital of Nevada.
cart	kaht	
Carter, Jimmy	Kah-tuh, Jim-ē	39th President of the US.
carton	kah-tun	
cart wheel	kaht wē-ul	
carve	kahv	
case	kās	
cashmere	kash-mē-uh	
cast iron	kast ī-un	
catcher	kach-uh	
cater	kā-tuh	
caterpillar	kat-uh-pil-uh	
catheter	kath-uh-tuh	
catty-cornered	katē-kaw-nud	In Maine, I have never heard this situation called "catty" cornered. (nor in NH) It's always pronounced "kitty" cornered. Kitē-kaw-nud.
cauterize	kawt-uh-rīz	
caviar	kav-ē-ah	
chagrin	shuh-grin	
chance	1) chahns 2) chans	Both are acceptable, but you will most often hear "chahns".
chancellor	chan-suh-luh	
chaperon	shap-uh-rōn	
char	chah	

charm	chahm	
carter	chah-tuh	
cheddar	ched-uh	Cheese.
Cherokee	Chār-uh-kē	Native North American tribe, now chiefly located in the states of Oklahoma and North Carolina.
cherub	chā-rub	1) A kind of angel. 2) A child with a sweet, innocent face.
Cheyenne	Shī-an	Capital of Wyoming, USA – also the name of a Native North American tribe.
chigger	chig-uh	They're red larva of some mites whose bite itches severely.
Colorado	Kawl-uh-rah-dō	State in the USA (CO). Capital: Denver.
crevasse	krev-ahs	
crier	krī-uh	
crime	krīm	
critter	krit-uh	
crooked	krook-ed	
cropper	krop-uh	
cross bar	kros bah	
cross fire	kros fī-uh	
croupier	krōōp-ē-uh	
crow bar	krō bah	
crozier	krō-"zh"-uh	
crucify	krōōs-i-fī	
cruel	krōō-ul	
cruiser	krōōz-uh	

cruller	krul-uh	
crupper	kr$\overline{oo}$p-uh	
cry	kr$\bar{\imath}$	
cucumber	ky$\overline{oo}$-kum-buh	
Cumberland	Kum-buh-lund	County in Maine.
curator	kyur-$\bar{a}$-tuh	
cursor	kur-suh	
cuspidor	kus-puh-d$\bar{o}$-uh	
cuss (slang)	kus	Not in Webster's. It describes words for swearing – any swear word.
cussed	kus-ed	Something very aggravating and frustrating. It could even be considered mean.
customer	kus-tum-uh	
cutter	cut-uh	
cybernetics	s$\bar{\imath}$-buh-net-ix	
cyberpunk	s$\bar{\imath}$-buh punk	
cyberspace	s$\bar{\imath}$-buh sp$\bar{a}$s	
cylinder	sil-un-duh	
cypher	s$\bar{\imath}$-fuh	
czar	zah	

Fourth letter of the English Alphabet D,d (dē)

Word	Pronunciation Examples	Notes
dagger	dag-uh	
dagnabbit (slang)	dag-nab-it	Example: Fred went to open a can of dog food for his faithful friend. Suddenly, the can opener broke, and he didn't have another one. "Dagnabbit!" he exclaimed. You see, it <u>is</u> an expression of exasperation.
dahlia	1) dal-ē-uh 2) dal-yuh	
dairy	dā-rē	
Dalai Lama	Dah-lē Lah-muh	A high priest of Lamaism.
damper	dam-puh	
dander	dan-duh	
danger	dānj-uh	
dangerous	dānj-rus	
dapper	dap-uh	Dressed stylishly.
Dardanelles	Dah-duh-nelz	A strait separating the Balkan peninsula from Asia Minor.
dare	dā-uh	
dare devil	dā-uh dev-ul	A bold person with little or no concern for safety.
daring	dār-in'	
dark	dahk	
Dark Ages	Dahk Ājez	The middle ages in Europe from AD 476 -1450.
darken	dahk-un	

dark horse	dahk hos	
darling	dah-lin'	
darn	dahn	1) To mend or repair a sock or clothing by sewing up a hole. 2) (slang) Another word for damn but not as bad.
dart	daht	
Darwin, Charles	Dah-win, Chahlz	Originated the theory of evolution.
dash board	dash bō-ud	
dashiki	dah-shē-kē	
dastardly	das-tud-lē	
data	1) data 2) dah-tuh	
daughter	daw-tuh	
davenport	dav-en-pō-ut	
day care	dā kā-uh	
dead head	ded hed	You remove the "head" of the flower when the bloom has gone by.
deal	dē-ul	
dealer ship	dē-ul-uh ship	
dear	1) dē-uh 2) dē-ah	A very common term used to convey respect and affection to a friend.
Dear John letter	Dē-uh Jawn let-uh	A letter written by one of two people in a love relationship with the purpose of breaking up the relationship.
debacle	dē-bawk-ul	
debar	dē-bah	
debark	dē-bahk	
debarkation	dē-bahk-ā-shun	

debauchery	dē-boch-uh-rē	
debit card	debit kahd	
debonair	deb-on-ā-uh	
debtor	1) det-uh 2) det-ah	
debutante	1) deb-yōō-taunt 2) deb-yōō-tahnt	
decanter	dē-kant-uh	
decelerate	dē-sel-uh-rāt	
December	Dē-sem-buh	
decided	duh-sīd-ed	WDE: duh-sawīd-ed
decipher	dē-sī-fuh	
declaration	dek-luh-rā-shun	
declare	dē-klā-uh	
décor	deh-kō-uh	
decorum	duh-kawr-um	
deep fry	dēp frī	WDE: dēp frawī
deer	dē-uh	
defile	dē-fī-ul	
defogger	dē-fog-uh	
deform	dē-fawm	
deformity	dē-fawm-uh-tē	
Delaware	Del-uh-wā-uh	State of the East US. (DE) Capital: Dover.
deliberate	1) dē-lib-uh-rit 2) duh-lib-rit	

deliver	1) dē-liv-uh 2) duh-liv-uh	
delivery	1) dē-liv-uh-rē 2) duh-liv-rē	
demarcation	dē-mahk-ā-shun	
demeanor	duh-mēn-uh	
demise	duh-mīz	
Democratic Party	Demōkrat-ik Paht-ē	
demographic	dem-ō-grahf-ik	
demography	demog-ruhf-ē	
demure	1) dem-yōor 2) duh-myōo-uh	
denier	1) de-nī-uh 2) duh-nī-uh	
denim	den-um	
Denmark	Den-mahk	Country in North Europe and islands in the North and Baltic Seas.
denominator	dē-nawm-in-ā-tuh	
denser	dens-uh	
denuclearize	dē-nōōk-lē-uh-rīz	
Denver	Den-vuh	Capital of Colorado.
depart	dē-paht	
departed	dē-paht-id	
department	dē-paht-munt	
department store	dē-paht-munt stō-uh	
departure	dē-pah-chuh	
deplore	dē-plō-uh	

deport	dē-pō-ut	
derail	dē-rā-ul	
derelict	dār-uh-likt	
dereliction	dār-uh-lik-shun	
derriere	dār-ē-ā-uh	Back end.
derringer	dār-in-juh	Small pistol.
desert	dez-ut	Hot, dry wilderness.
deserted	dez-ert-ed	Abandoned.
design	1) duh-zīn 2) dez-īn	
desire	1) dez-ī-uh 2) dē-zī-uh	
Des Moines	Duh Mō-ēn	Capital of Iowa.
despair	des-pā-uh	
desperate	des-prit	
desperation	des-puh-rā-shun	
dessert	1) duh-zert 2) dē-zurt	
destroyer	duh-strōē-yuh	
deter	dē-ter	
detergent	1) dē-ter-jent 2) duh-turj-unt	
detour	dē-tō-uh	
detractor	dē-trak-tuh	
Deuteronomy	Dōō-tuh-rawn-umē	
deutsche mark	1) dō-ech mahk 2) dōōch mahk	

devil-may-care	dev-ul-mā-kā-uh	Careless attitude.
devour	1) duh-vow-uh 2) dev-ow-uh	
dexterous	dex-trus	
dial	dī-al	
diameter	dī-am-eh-tuh	
diaper	dī-uh-puh	
dicker	dik-uh	
dictator	dik-tā-tuh	
diddle	did-ul	The dictionary says "to waste (time) in trifling" – but it depends upon the attitude of the one who is considered to be diddelin'. Also can be a sexual connotation.
die hard	dī hahd	
differ	dif-uh	
diagraph	dī-uh-grahf	
Dijon Mustard	Dē-jon Mus-tud	
dime store	dīm stō-uh	They were also called "Five & Ten" cent stores. One would be hard put to find one these days. You'd be more likely to find the "Dollar Store" or "Dollar General".
dimmer	dim-uh	
diner	dīn-uh	
dinner	din-uh	
dinner ware	din-uh wā-uh	
dinosaur	1) dī-nuh-sō-uh 2) dī-nō-saw	
dipper	dip-uh	
dire	dī-uh	

director	dī-rek-tuh
dirt poor	dert pō-uh
disappear	dis-uh-pē-uh
disarm	dis-ahm
disaster	1) dis-astuh 2) diz-astuh
disbar	dis-bah
discard	dis-cahd
discharge	dis-chahj
disclaimer	dis-clām-uh
discolor	dis-cul-ah
discomfort	dis-cum-fut
discard	dis-cahd
discover	dis-kuv-uh
discovery	dis-cov-uh-rē
disembark	dis-em-bahk
disencumber	dis-en-cum-buh
disfavor	dis-fā-vuh
disfigure	dis-fig-yuh
disgorge	dis-gawj
dishearten	dis-hah-ten
dishonor	dis-awn-uh
dishwasher	dish-waw-shuh
disinformation	dis-in-fawm-ā-shun
disinterested	dis-intuh-rest-ed

disintermediation	dis-intuh-mēd-ē-ā-shun	
dismember	dis-mem-buh	
disorder	dis-aw-duh	
disorderly	dis-aw-duh-lē	
disorganize	dis-aw-gun-īz	
disport	disp-ō-ut	
disregard	dis-rē-gahd	
disrepair	dis-rē-pā-uh	
dissertation	dis-uh-tā-shun	
dissever	disev-uh	
dissimilar	dis-simil-uh	
distemper	dis-temp-uh	
distort	1) distawt 2) dis-tō-ut	A very small amount.
distributor	dis-trib-yo͞o-tuh	
dite	dīt	
dither	di-"th"-uh	
ditto mark	dit-ō mahk	WDE: div-awīd
divers	dī-vuz	
divide	div-īd	
divining rod	divīnin' rod	
divisor	divī-zuh	
divorce	div-ō-us	
divorcee	1) div-ō-us-ā 2) div-ō-us-ē	
Doberman	Dōb-uh-mun	

dock yard	dok-yahd	
doctor	dok-tuh	
doer	dōō-uh	
dog ear	daug ē-uh	
dog eared	daug ē-ud	Not the ear of a dog but, rather, a corner of a page of a book folded down to mark a page.
do gooder	dōō gud-uh	A person who takes great pleasure in helping other people, a lot.
dog tired	dawg tī-ud	A loyal dog will go or work for its master until it's so tired it can hardly bare its weight to walk- near exhaustion.
dollar	dawl-uh	
domineer	dom-in-ē-uh	To rule over. Webster's says "to rule over in a harsh way." I disagree with that definition. After all, there are many situations when someone needs to take charge – to domineer – it isn't a bad thing. But dependin' on the personality of the one who's domineering, it can be a harsh or uncomfortable situation.
donor	dōn-uh	
doodler	dōō-dul-uh	Someone who enjoys rather aimless sketchin'.
dormer	dawm-uh	
dorsal	daw-sul	
dory	1) daw-rē 2) dor-ē	
dosimeter	dō-sim-uh-tuh	
dotard	dot-ud	A word used for an old, old person who has regressed to behaving quite childishly.
double boiler	dub-ul boēl-uh	
double crosser	dub-ul kros-uh	A person that was trusted to do something or to keep a secret but failed that trust.

double decker	dub-ul dek-ah	Anything where the base has a second layer.
double header	dub-ul hed-uh	
double standard	dub-ul stand-ud	
dour	dow-uh	Another way to describe a dour person is a "sober-sides" or a "pickle" of a person.
Dover	Dō-vuh	Capital city of Delaware.
dowager	dow-uh-juh	An elderly wealthy woman who got her good fortune from their dead husband.
dower	dow-uh	A man's property that is left to his wife.
Down East	Down Ēst	In New England, especially Maine, according to Webster's fourth edition. See page three of this book's introduction.
downer	down-uh	1) A sad or unpleasant experience. 2) (slang) A drug that causes a "high" with some measure of sedation.
down hearted	down haht-ed	Very sad, maybe depressed.
down pour	down pō-uh	A steady, heavy rain.
down stairs	down stā-uz	Going down to a lower floor.
downward	down wud	
dowser	dowz-uh	One able to use a divinin' rod, usually successfully.
draft	drahft	A real Mainer would always pronounce that "a" as in "ah" in draft.
drafty	drahft-ē	
drama	drah-muh	Serious, rivetin' performance or experience.
draper	drā-puh	
draperies	drāp-rēz	
drawer	1) draw 2) drawr-uh	

drawers	drawz	
drawing board	draw-rin' bō-ud	
drawing card	draw-rin' kahd	
drawl	drawl	A way of speaking so that the tempo is fairly slow and the vowels are drawn out. Examples: 1) Slow Southern US drawl. 2) Sexy Texan drawl.
drawn butter	drawn but-uh	
dresser	des-uh	A chest of drawers.
drier	drī-uh	WDE: drawī-uh
drill master	1) dril mast-uh 2) dril mahst-uh	
drive	drīv	WDE: drawīv
drive shaft	drīv shahft	
dropper	drop-uh	
drover	drōv-uh	
drug store	drug stō-uh	
drum major	drum mā-juh	
drunkard	drunk-ud	
dry	drī	WDE: drawī
dry cleaner	drī clēn-uh	
DST	No change.	Daylight Savings Time.
dub	dub	In Maine, it's not unusual to hear someone being called "a dub" when the person is irresponsible, disappointing and possibly a liar. If they are all these, they are a real dub.
Dublin	No change.	Capital of Ireland.

85

ducky	duk-ē	Means delightful, everything is just right.
duffer	duf-uh	The definition of a duffer in Maine doesn't coincide with what Webster's has written. In Maine, there are little duffers. That is, a small child who is loveable and is affectionately called a duffuh. Then, you have your old duffer – that is a somewhat scruffy older fellow who is quite cordial and most likeable.
DUI	No change.	This is an abbreviation for a citation for driving under the influence of alcohol or drugs.
dulcimer	dul-sim-uh	
dullard	dul-ud	A person lackin' much of any mental capacity.
dumb waiter	dum wā-tuh	
dumper (slang)	dump-uh	A container for dumping rubbish of all kinds.
dumpling	dump-lin'	1) Boiled dough in sauce or gravy and served with some kind of meat 2) Term of affection for some special person or to describe an adorable, darling child.
dumpster	dump-stuh	A large metal trash and rubbish bin. It gets emptied into a truck and eventually taken away, once again leaving the dumpster empty.
dura mater	dur-uh mat-uh	Tough membrane covering the brain and spinal cord.
duster	dust-uh	
Dutch Door	Duch Dō-uh	
dwarf	dw-awf	Smaller than "normal" size – or a little magical person.

Fifth letter of the English Alphabet E,e (ē)

Word	Pronunciation Examples	Notes
eager	ē-guh	
ear	ē-uh	
ear mark	ē-uh mahk	
earthen ware	urthen wā-uh	
earthward	urth-wud	
Easter	Ē-stuh	Spring celebration of the resurrection of Jesus Christ, Almighty God's son.
easterly	ēst-uh-lē	
eastern	ēst-un	
easterner	ēst-un-uh	
Eastern Hemisphere	Ēst-un Hem-is-fē-uh	
Eastern Standard Time	Ēst-un Stand-ud Tīm	WDE: Ēst-un Stand-ud Tawīm (EST)
east ward	ēst wud	
easy chair	ēzē chā-uh	
eat	1) ēt 2) et	Many old timers or farmers or deep coastal folks say "et" instead of ēt.
éclair	ē-klā-uh	
economize	ēkon-um-īz	
Ecuador	Ek-wauh-dō-uh	Country on the Southwest coast of South America.
editor	ed-i-tuh	
editor in chief	ed-i-tuh in chēf	

effervesce	ef-uh-ves	
effort	ef-ut	
egg beater	eg bēt-uh	
eider	ī-duh	
eider down	ī-duh down	
Eisenhower, Dwight David	Īzen-how-uh, Dwīt David	39th President of the United States.
either	1) ē-"th"-uh 2) ī-"th"-uh	
elastic	e-lahs-tik	Never e-las-tik. Occasionally, you do hear the "long ē" at the beginning of elastic.
elasticize	e-lahs-tuh-sīz	
elder	el-duh	
elder berry	el-duh ber-ē	
elderly	el-duh-lē	
El Dorado	El Daw-rahd-ō	Any place supposed to be rich in gold.
electioneer	1) uh-lek-shun-ē-uh 2) ē-lek-shun-ē-uh	
elector	1) uh-lekt-uh 2) ē-lek-tuh	
electric chair	1) uh-lek-trik chā-uh 2) ē-lek-trik chā-uh	
electrify	1) uh-lek-truh-fī 2) ē-lek-truh-fī	
electrocardiogram	ē-lek-trō-kahd-ē-ō-gram	
electrocardiograph	ē-lek-trō-kahd-ē-ō-grahf	
elementary particle	el-uh-men-tuh-rē pah-tik-ul	

elevator	el-uh-vā-tuh	
elite	1) uh-lēt 2) ē-lēt	
elixir	1) ē-lix-uh 2) uh-lix-uh	
El Paso	El Pah-sō	City in western Texas.
El Salvador	El Sal-vuh-dō-uh	Country in Central America on the Pacific Ocean.
elsewhere	els-wā-uh	
embargo	em-bah-gō	
embark	em-bahk	
ember	em-buh	
embroider	em-brōēd-uh	
Emerson, Ralph Waldo	Em-uh-sun, Ralf Wawl-dō	A United States writer and philosopher 1803-1882.
emery	em-rē	
emery board	em-rē bō-ud	
emir	uh-mē-uh	A ruler or prince in Muslim Countries.
emperor	1) em-puh-ruh 2) emp-ur-uh	An empire's supreme ruler.
empire	em-pī-uh	
employer	em-plōē-uh	
empower	em-pow-uh	
enamor	en-am-uh	
enclosure	en-klō-"zh"-uh	
encore	on-kō-uh	
encounter	en-cown-tuh	

encumber	en-cum-buh
endanger	en-dānj-uh
endangered	en-dānj-ud
endear	en-dē-uh
endearment	en-dē-uh-ment
endeavor	en-dev-uh
endorse	en-dō-us
endure	en-dōō-uh
endurance	en-dur-uns
energetic	en-uh-jet-ik
energize	en-uh-jīz
energy	en-uh-jē
enervate	en-uh-vāt
enforce	en-fō-us
engender	en-jen-duh
engineer	en-jen-ē-uh
engineering	en-jin-ēr-in'
English horn	Inglish hawn
engorge	en-gawj
engraving	en-grāv-in'
enlarge	en-lahj
enormity	e-naw-mi-tē
enormous	1) ē-naw-mus 2) uh-naw-mus
enquire	en-qwī-uh

enquiring	en-qwī-uh-rin'	
enrapture	en-rap-chuh	
enshrine	en-shrīn	
ensnare	en-snā-uh	
ensure	en-sh$\overline{oo}$-uh	
enter	en-tuh	
enterprise	en-tuh-prīz	WDE: en-tuh-prawīz
entertain	en-tuh-tān	
entertaining	en-tuh-tān-in'	
entertainment	en-tuh-tān-munt	
enth degree	enth duh-grē	If one person has annoyed another until they cannot tolerate it, they have pushed to the enth degree.
entire	en-tī-uh	
entwine	en-twīn	
epicenter	epē-sen-tuh	
epicure	epē-kyoo	
epigraph	epē-grahf	
epitaph	1) epē-taf 2) epe-tahf	
Epstein-Barr	Epstīn-Bah	A herpes-like virus that causes mononucleosis, infections, and may cause some forms of cancer as well as a paralytic syndrome named for it.
equator	ē-kwā-tuh	
equine	ē-kwīn	
erase	1) ē-rās 2) uh-rās	

eraser	1) uh-rās-uh 2) ē-rās-uh	
erect	1) ē-rekt 2) uh-rekt	
Erin	Ār-in	Old poetic name for Ireland.
error	ār-uh	
escalator	esk-uh-lā-tuh	
escort	esk-ō-ut	
escritoire	es-kri-twah	A writing desk.
ESP	ekstra sen-suh-rē puh-sep-shun	Extra Sensory Perception. Able to perceive the unusual via heightened senses.
espalier	espal-ē-uh	
esprit de corps	es-prē duh kor	
esquire	es-kwī-uh	In the US, it's a title used by lawyers. In England, it ranks just below a knight.
EST	Ēstun Stand-ud Tīm	WDE: Ēstun Stand-ud Tawīm Eastern Standard Time.
ester	es-tuh	Organic compound.
Esther	Est-uh	Jewess who saved her people from slaughter and became the wife of a Persian king.
estuary	est-yōō-ārē	
ET	Ēstun Tīm	WDE: Ēstun Tawīm Eastern Time.
ether	ēth-uh	
euchre	yōō-kuh	A card game
even tempered	ē-vun temp-ud	Easy going.
ever	ev-uh	

Everest, Mount	Ev-rest, Mount	Highest known mountain. Part of the Himalayas.
everglade	evuh-glād	
ever green	evuh grēn	A tree or shrub that stays green year round.
ever lasting	1) ev-uh lastin' 2) ev-uh-lahs-tin'	
ever more	ev-uh mō-uh	
everywhere	ev-rē-wā-uh	
evil doer	ēv-ul dōō-uh	
ewer	yōō-uh	A large water pitcher with a wide mouth.
exacerbate	eks-as-uh-bāt	To make more intense.
exaggerate	eks-aj-uh-rāt	
exasperate	eks-as-puh-rāt	To cause frustration to the point of anger.
excelsior	ek-sel-sē-aw	
executer	1) ek-se-kyōō-tuh 2) eks-uh-kyōō-tuh	
exemplar	eks-emp-luh	
exercise	eks-uh-sīz	
exhort	1) eks-awt 2) eks-ō-ut	
exonerate	eks-on-uh-rāt	
exorbitant	eks-aw-buh-tunt	
exorcise	eks-aw-sīz	
expectorate	ek-speck-tuh-rāt	
expediter	eks-puh-dīt-uh	
explore	ek-splō-uh	

export	ek-spō-ut
exporter	1) eks-pawt-uh 2) ek-spō-ut-uh
expositor	ek-spawz-uh-taw-rē
expository	eks-pawz-uh-tor-ē
extempore	eks-temp-aw-rē Occurs without preparation.
extended care	ek-stend-ed kā-uh
exterior	ek-stēr-ē-uh
exterminator	eks-term-in-āt-uh
extort	1) ek-stawt 2) ek-stō-uht
extortion	ek-staw-shun
extracurricular	ek-struh-kur-ik-yōō-luh
exuberant	eks-ōō-buh-runt
eye catcher	ī kach-uh
eye glass	ī glahs
eye opener	ī ōpun-uh
eye sore	ī sō-uh
eye wear	ī wā-uh

Sixth letter of the English Alphabet F,f (ef)

Word	Pronunciation Examples	Notes
factor	fak-tuh	
factory	fak-tuh-rē	
failing	fā-ul-in'	

failure	fā-ul-yuh	
fair	fā-uh	1) Attractive. 2) Clear and sunny. 3) Just/honest. 4) Not foul (in baseball). 5) Regular, often historical, gathering of folks to sell or buy goods, go on various rides, see livestock, competition for best livestock or baked goods, etc.
Fairbanks	Fā-uh-banks	City in Alaska
fair game	fā-uh gām	
fair haired	fā-uh hā-ud	
fairly	fā-ul-lē	
falling star	fawlin' stah	
falter	fawl-tuh	
familiar	fum-il-ē-uh	
familiarize	fuh-mil-ē-uh-rīz	
family practitioner	fam-lē prak-tish-un-uh	
fancier	fan-sē-uh	
fanfare	fan-fā-uh	
far	fah	
far away	fah uh-wā	
farce	fahs	Something ridiculous.
fare	fā-uh	
farewell	fā-uh wel	
far fetched	fah fechtd	
far flung	fah flung	
farm	fahm	
farmer	fahm-uh	

95

farming	fahm-in'	
farm yard	fahm yahd	
Ferrier	Fār-ē-uh	Takes care of a horse's hooves, shoeing, etc.
fart	faht	1) One can <u>do</u> a fart – that is, flatus (gas from the rectum). 2) One can <u>be</u> a "fart", meaning a stubborn, irritating soul. 3) An old fart – one who is ornery, frustratin' and can be quite disagreeable. 4) If a friend calls you a "fart" or an "old fart", don't take offense. They are just referrin' to you bein' temporarily out of sorts.
farther	1) fah-"th"-uh 2) fur-"th"-uh	
farthest	1) fah-"th"-ist 2) fah-"th"-est	Further than further.
fast	fahst	Rarely, some will say fa-sen.
fasten	fah-sun	
fast forward	fahst faw-wud	
fast talk	fahst tawk	
favor	fā-vuh	
favorite	fāv-rit	
favoritism	fāv-ruh-tizm	
fealty	fē-ul-tē	Loyalty.
fear	fē-uh	
fearful	fē-uh-ful	
feather	fe-"th"-uh	
February	Feb-yōō-āry	For some reason, we usually leave out the first "r" in our pronunciation.

federal	fed-rul	The middle "er" is ignored for some reason. It just amazes me that we Mainers learned to spell correctly <u>at all</u>!
federalize	fed-rul-īz	
federation	fed-uh-rā-shun	
fedora	1) fed-aw-ruh 2) fuh-dawr-uh	
feeler	fē-ul-uh	
feldspar	feld-spah	
feline	fē-līn	WDE: fē-lawīn
fellow traveler	fel-ō trav-ul-uh	
female	fē-mā-ul	
fencing	fens-in'	Almost always drop the "g" from the "ing".
fender	fen-duh	
ferment	fur-ment	
ferret	fār-et	
Ferris wheel	Fār-is wē-ul	
fertilizer	fur-til-īz-uh	
fervor	fur-vuh	
fester	fest-uh	
fetching	fech-in'	
fetter	fet-uh	
fever	fē-vuh	
fever blister	fē-vuh blist-uh	
fibber	fib-uh	One who tells minor, hopefully harmless lies.

fiber	fī-buh	
fiber board	fī-buh bō-ud	
fiber glass	fī-buh glahs	Not gl<u>a</u>s.
fidelity	1) fuh-del-i-tē 2) fī-del-uh-tē	Either way, it is a word recognizable as meanin': 1) To be faithful or dedicated. 2) Accurate and sound reproduction.
field	fē-uld	
field glasses	fē-uld glahs-es	
field marshal	fē-uld mah-shal	
fierce	fē-us	
fiery	fī-uh-rē	Means – like fire; glaring hot flames.
fighter	fīt-uh	
figurine	fig-yuh-rēn	
file	fī-ul	
filibuster	fil-uh-bus-tuh	
Fillmore, Millard	Fill-mō-uh, Mil-ud	13th president of the USA.
filter	fil-tuh	
fine art	fīn aht	
finery	1) fīn-uh-rē 2) fīn-rē	
finger	fing-uh	
finger board	fing-uh bō-uhd	
finger nail	fing-uh nā-ul	
finnen haddie	fin-in had-ē	Haddock, smoked to make a unique flavor.
fiord	fē-awd	A deep inlet of the ocean with high cliffs on each side. There is one called Somes Sound on Mount Desert Island, Maine. They are rare on the east coast of the USA.

fire	fī-uh	
fire arm	fī-uh ahm	
fire cracker	fī-uh krak-uh	
fire fighter	fī-uh fīt-uh	
fire storm	fī-uh stawm	
fire tower	fī-uh tow-uh	
fire water	fī-uh wah-tuh	
fire works	fī-uh werx	
firstborn	ferst bawn	
fisher	fish-uh	
fisherman	fish-uh-mun	
fishery	fish-uh-rē	
fissure	fish-uh	
five star	fīv stah	An excellent rating for a restaurant or motel.
fixings	fix-inz'	This refers to all the salads, vegetables, breads and stuffings, as well as all the desserts that go along with the meat dishes in a holiday or celebration feast.
flabbergast (slang)	flab-uh-gast	Being so surprised or amazed that one is practically speechless or dumbfounded with surprise.
flair	flā-uh	1) A striking attractive sense of style. 2) A natural talent to do something.
flame thrower	flām thrō-uh	
Flanders	Flan-duz	A region in France and Belgium.
flapper	flap-uh	
flare up	flā-uh up	

flash forward	flash faw-wud	
flat car	flat kah	
flat iron	flat ī-un	
flatter	flat-uh	
flatware	flat-wā-uh	
flatworm	flat-werm	
flavor	flā-vuh	
flea market	flē mahk-et	
flicker	flik-uh	
flier	flī-uh	
flip chart	flip chaht	
flipper	flip-uh	
floor	flō-uh	
floor board	flō-uh bō-ud	
flora	flaw-ruh	
floral	flaw-rul	
florid	flaw-rid	
Florida	Flaw-ruh-duh	Southern US state. (FL) Capital: Tallahassee.
florin	flaw-rin	
florist	flaw-rist	
flounder	flown-duh	1) Flat fish caught for food, such as halibut. 2) Struggle without progress. 3) Talking without being able to make your point.
flourish	flour-ish	
flow chart	flō chaht	

flower	flow-uh	
flowerpot	flow-uh pot	
flowery	flow-uh-rē	
fluorocarbon	flur-ō-kah-bun	
flurry	flur-ē	
fluster	flust-uh	
flustered	flust-uhd	Frazzled, frustrated.
flutter	flut-uh	
fly	flī	WDE: flawī
fly by night	flī bī nīt	Someone making an attempt at doing something that they really don't know how to do AND they don't have any directions.
fly by wire	flī bī wī-uh	
fly catcher	flī kach-uh	
flier	flī-uh	
flying colors	flī-in' kuluz	Accomplished a task exceptionally well.
flying saucer	flī-in' saw-suh	
fly paper	flī pā-puh	
fodder	fawd-uh	
fog horn	fawg hawn	A "horn" that blows to warn ships of rocks or some hazard – most often used in foul or foggy weather.
folder	fold-uh	
folk lore	fōk lō-uh	A particular culture's legends and traditional beliefs.
follower	fawl-ō-uh	
food processor	food praw-ses-uh	

fool hardy	fool had-ē	Without taking care – reckless or daring.
foot locker	foot lok-uh	
foot path	foot pahth	
foot sore	foot sō-uh	
foot wear	foot wā-uh	
foot work	foot werk	
for	1) faw 2) fō-uh	Pronunciation depends on the situation.
forage	faw-rij	
forbear	1) fō-uh-bā-uh 2) faw-bā-uh	
force	fō-us	
forced	fō-usd	
ford	fō-ud	Shallow place in a stream where it's easy to cross.
Ford, Gerald R. Jr.	Fō-ud, Jār-uld Ah. Jōōn-yah	38th president of the USA.
fore	fō-uh	
fore and aft	fō-uh and ahft	From the bow to the stern of the boat.
forearm	fō-uh ahm	The arm between the wrist and elbow.
fore bear	fō-uh bā-uh	
fore father	fō-uh fah-"th"-uh	
forego	fō-uh gō	
forefinger	fō-uh-fing-uh	Index finger.
foreign	faw-run	
foreign born	faw-ren bawn	
foreigner	faw-ren-uh	

foreign minister	faw-run min-uh-stuh	
foreknow	fō-uh nō	
forelock	fō-uh lok	Hair growin' just above the forehead that flops down, like on a horse.
foreman	1) fō-uh-mun 2) faw-mun	
former	faw-muh	
form letter	fawm let-uh	
fornication	faw-ni-kā-shun	An unmarried person havin' sexual intercourse.
for swear	faw swā-uh	
fort	fō-ut	
forte	faw-tā	
fourth	fō-uth	
forthright	fō-uth rīt	
fortify	faw-ti-fī	
Fort Knox	Fō-ut Nox	1) Is on the Penobscot River in Bucksport, ME at the mouth of the river. 2) Of course, there is the Fort Knox in Kentucky, where the gold reserve is.
fort night	fō-ut nīt	A span of time lasting two weeks.
fortress	faw-tres	
fortuitous	faw-tōo-i-tus	
fortunate	faw-chōon-it	
fortune	faw-chōon	
fortune teller	faw-chōon tel-uh	
forty	faw-tē	
forward	faw-wud	

foster	faws-tuh	
founder	fown-duh	
four	fō-uh	
four flusher	fō-uh flush-uh	
four score	fō-uh skō-uh	Four times twenty (eighty).
four square	fō-uh skw-ā-uh	
fourth	fō-uth	
fourth class	fō-uth klahs	
Fourth of July	Fō-uh ov Jōolī	
fox terrier	fox tār-ē-uh	
Frankfort	Frank-fut	
frankfurter	frank-fut-uh	Hot dog.
Franklin	Frank-lin	A county in Maine.
Franklin, Benjamin	Frank-lin Ben-juh-min	1706-1790. Great statesman, scientist, inventor and writer.
free booter	frē bōot-uh	
free form	frē fawm	
free loader	frē lōd-uh	
free on board	frē on bō-ud	
freezer	frē-zuh	
freighter	frāt-uh	
French doors	French dō-uz	
French horn	French hawn	
fresh water	fresh wo-tuh	
friar	frī-ah	

frig (slang)	frig	A real bother – a pain in the neck!
fritter	frit-uh	
from	frawm	
frontier	frunt-ē-uh	
front runner	frunt run-uh	
frosting	frost-in'	
forward	faw-wud	
frozen custard	frō-zen kus-tud	
Fryeburg Fair	Frī-burg Fā-uh	Oldest fair in Maine – held on the western border, near NH.
fryer	frī-uh	
full bore	ful bō-uh	
full scale	1) ful skā-l 2) ful skā-ul	
fund raiser	fund rā-zuh	
funeral	1) fyo͞on-uh-rul 2) fyo͞on-rul	
funicular	fyo͞o-nik-yo͞o-luh	A type of mountain railway.
funny farm	funē fahm	
furniture	1) fur-nuh-cho͞o-uh 2) fur-ni-chō-uh	
furor	fēyur-uh	
furrier	fur-ē-uh	
further	fur-"th"-uh	
furthermore	fur-"th"-uh-mō-uh	
fusilier	fyo͞o-zil-ē-uh	Soldier armed with a flintlock musket.

Seventh letter of the English Alphabet G.g (jē)

Word	Pronunciation Examples	Notes
gabardine	gab-uh-dēn	
Gabriel	Gāb-rē-ul	One of the archangels in the Bible.
gaffer	gaf-uh	In charge of lights on stage.
gainer	gā-nuh	A fancy dive.
gaiter	gā-tuh	
gale	gā-ul	
gallbladder	gawl-blad-uh	
gallery	gal-uh-rē	
galore	guh-lō-uh	
galvanometer	gal-vuh-nom-i-tuh	
game keeper	gām kēp-uh	
gamester	gām-stuh	
gander	gan-duh	1) A male goose. 2) Taking a long, close look.
gangster	gang-stuh	
gar	gah	A freshwater fish.
garage	guh-rahj	
garb	gahb	
garbage	gah-bij	
garble	gah-bul	
garcon	gah-sōn	A waiter.
garden	gah-dun	
gardenia	gah-dēn-yuh	

garden variety	gah-den vuh-rī-uh-tē	
Garfield, James	Gah-fēld, Jāmz	20th president of the USA.
gargantuan	gah-gan-chōō-un	
gargoyle	gah-gō-ē-ul	
garland	gah-lund	
garlic	gah-lik	
garment	gah-munt	
garner	gah-nuh	
garnet	gah-net	
garnish	gah-nish	
garnishment	gah-nish-munt	
garret	gār-it	An attic. Pronounce the "r".
garter	gah-tuh	
gas chamber	gas chām-buh	
gas mask	1) gas mahsk 2) gas mask	
gate crasher	gāt krash-uh	
gather	ga-"th"-uh	
gator	gāt-uh	
gawm	No change.	This is a clumsy, accident-prone person.
gawmgutchet	No change.	Similar to a gawm but even worse – but more hopeless, even more of a fumbler and terribly clumsy.
gazetteer	gaz-uh-tē-uh	Dictionary or index of names.
gear	gē-uh	
geezer	gē-zuh	Odd or eccentric older man.

Geiger counter	Gī-guh kount-uh	
gendarme	"zh"-on-dahm	A French policeman.
gender	jen-duh	
gendered	jen-dud	
general	jen-rul	
generalissimo	jen-rul-is-im-ō	
general practitioner	jen-rul prak-ti-shun-uh	
generator	jen-uh-rā-tuh	
genteel	jen-tē-ul	Was taught to be very polite.
gentile	jen-tī-ul	Anyone not a Jew.
George III	Jawj thuh third	Lived 1738-1820.
Georgia	Jaw-juh	Southern state in the USA. (GA) Capital: Atlanta.
German Shepherd	Jer-mun Shep-ud	The most intelligent of the dog world, many believe.
gerrymander	jer-ē-mand-uh	Has to do with the governor of MA in 1812, about voting.
gesture	jes-chuh	
get together	get to-ge-"th"-uh	
geyser	gī-zuh	
ghost writer	gōst rīt-uh	
gibber	jib-uh	Nonsense talk.
gibberish	jib-uh-rish	Baby talk.
Gibraltar	Juh-brawl-tuh	British, but at the southern tip of Spain.
Gila monster	Hēl-uh mon-stuh	Poisonous, rather big lizard of the SW US deserts.

ginger	jin-juh	
ginger ale	1) jin-juh ā-ul 2) jin-juh rā-ul	
girder	gurd-uh	
gizzard	giz-ud	
glacier	glā-shuh	
gladiator	glad-ē-ā-tuh	
glare	glā-uh	
glass	glahs	Never gl<u>a</u>s.
glassware	glahs-wā-uh	
glazier	glā-"zh"-uh	
glider	glīd-uh	
glimmer	glim-uh	
glitter	glit-uh	
global warming	glōb-ul wawm-in'	
globe trotter	glōb trawt-uh	
globular	glōb-yōō-luh	
glower	glow-uh	To stare with anger.
gnarled	nah-ld	
goal keeper	gōl kēp-uh	
gobbler	gob-luh	A turkey.
god daughter	god daw-tuh	The female child that had you as responsible for her at her christening (and lifelong).
god father god mother	god fah-"th"-uh god muh-"th"-uh	A man and woman appointed as responsible for a child at the child's christening.
gofer	gō-fuh	

go getter	gō get-uh	
going over	1) gōin' ōv-uh 2) gō-ēn ōv-uh	
goiter	gō-ē-tuh	
golden ager	gōl-dun āj-uh	
gold standard	gōld stand-ud	
golly wobbles	gaw-lē wob-ulz	This can occur anytime there is high stress – good or bad. Symptoms are: 1) Legs feel weak and shaky. 2) Stomach is queasy or has butterflies. 3) Mind may be distracted, slow, or jittery.
good tempered	good temp-ud	
goose bumps	No change.	Little bumps that occur on the skin when one feels cold, afraid, or in an eerie situation. They are caused by the tiny muscles at the base of the hair follicles contracting – causing a goose bump.
gopher	gō-fuh	
gore	gō-uh	
gorge	gawj	
gorgeous	gawj-us	
gormandize	gaw-mun-dīz	To eat like a glutton.
gorp	gawp	A mixture of healthy foods, such as oats, nuts, raisins – eaten to get more energy.
gorse	gaws	The same as a furze. It's a prickly evergreen shrub native to Europe.
gossamer	gaws-um-uh	
gourd	gō-ud	
gourmand	goo-uh-mund	

gourmet	1) gō-uh-mā
	2) gaw-mā
govern	guv-un
governance	guv-un-uns
governess	guv-uh-nes
government	guv-un-ment
governor	guv-un-uh
graft	grahft
Grail	Grā-ul
grammar	gram-uh
granddaughter	grand-dawt-uh
grandeur	grand-juh
grandfather	grand-fah-"th"-uh
grand master	1) grand mast-uh
	2) grand mah-stuh
grandmother	grand-mu-"th"uh
Grant, Ulysses Simpson	No change. 18th president of the USA – was also a union commander in the Civil War.
granular	gran-yōō-luh
graphic	grahf-ik
graphite	grahf-īt
grasp	As written or grahsp.
grass	grahs
grasshopper	grahs hop-uh
grave yard	grāv yahd
gravimeter	grav-i-mēt-uh

grey matter	grā mat-uh	Nerve tissue of the brain and spinal cord – effects one's intellectual capacity.
great hearted	grāt hahted	
green grocer	grēn grōs-uh	Deals with fresh veggies and fruit.
green horn	grēn hawn	A naïve person with little, if any, experience.
green manure	grēn muh-noo-uh	
green pepper	grēn pep-uh	
green power	grēn pow-uh	
greeting card	grēt-in' kahd	
grenadier	gren-uh-dē-uh	A soldier who threw grenades.
grinder	grīn-duh	
grocer	grō-suh	
ground clover	grownd klōv-uh	
grounder	grownd-uh	In baseball, a ball that is hit and travels along the ground.
ground floor	grownd flō-uh	
ground glass	grownd glahs	
ground water	grownd wo-tuh	
grouper	groop-uh	
guesser	ges-uh	
guilder	gild-uh	
guitar	gi-tah	
gunfire	gun-fī-uh	
gunner	gun-uh	

gun powder	gun pow-duh
gusher	gush-uh
gutter	gut-uh

Eighth letter of the English Alphabet H,h (āch)

Word	Pronunciation Examples	Notes
habeouscorpus	hā-bē-us-kaw-pus	A detained person going before the court.
haber dasher	ha-buh dash-uh	
habit forming	hab-it fawm-in'	
ha-choo	No change.	Sound of a sneeze.
hacker	hak-uh	
haft	hahft	Hilt or handle of an axe or knife-type tool.
haggard	hag-ud	
hail storm	hā-ul stawm	
hair	hā-uh	
hair dresser	hā-uh dres-uh	
halberd	hal-burd	A combined spear and battle axe. (15th-16th century)
half	hahf	
half brother	hahf bru-"th"-uh	When one parent is different than that of a sibling.
half dollar	hahf dol-uh	
half hearted	hahf haht-ed	Little interest or effort in the point of interest.
half mast	hahf mahst	
half sister	hahf sis-tuh	When one parent is different than that of a sibling.

halibut	hawl-uh-but	Sometimes you hear a flat-lander call it a *hal*-uh-but. It is also called a flounder.
hallelujah	hal-ā-lōō-yuh	Literally, praise to Jehovah. "Jah" is short for Jehovah. It generally means praise to almighty God.
hallmark	haul-mahk	
halter	haul-tuh	
halve	hahv	
halyard	hal-yud	
hamburger	ham-burg-uh	
hammer	ham-uh	
hamper	ham-puh	
hamster	ham-stuh	
Hancock	Han-kawk	A county in Down East ME.
hand car	hand kah	
handicapper	handē-kap-uh	
handicraft	hand-ē-krahft	
handkerchief	hank-uh-chif	
handle bar	hand-ul bah	
hangar	hang-uh	Shelter for aircraft.
hanger	hang-uh	Something used to hang something else up.
hang over	hang ō-vuh	
haphazard	hap-hazud	
happy hour	hapē ow-uh	
hara-kiri	hār-ē-kār-ē	Ritual suicide.
harass	1) huh-ras 2) huh-rahs	

harbinger	hah-bin-juh	
harbor	hah-buh	
hard	hahd	
hard core	hahd kō-uh	
hard cover	hahd kuv-uh	
hard hearted	hahd haht-ed	
hard liner	hahd līn-uh	
hardly	hahd-lē	
hard ware	hahd wā-uh	
hare	hā-uh	
harem	hār-um	
hark	hahk	
harlot	hah-lut	
harm	hahm	
harmonic	hah-mawn-ik	
harmonica	hah-mawn-ik-uh	
harmonize	hah-mun-īz	
harmony	hah-mun-ē	
harp	hahp	
harpsichord	hahp-si-kawd	
harrier	hār-ē-uh	1) A small hound 2) A cross-country runner.
Harrisburg	Hār-is-burg	Capital of Pennsylvania.
harrow	hār-ō	To cause mental distress.
harrowing	hār-ō-in'	

harsh	hah-sh	
hart	haht	Red deer.
Hartford	Haht-fud	Capital of Connecticut.
harvest	hah-vest	
hasp	hasp	
hatter	hat-uh	Makes and cares for men's hats.
hauberk	hō-berk	Medieval coat of armor. High fashion for women.
haute couture	ōt k$\overline{oo}$-t$\overline{oo}$-uh	
Hawaii	Huh-wī-ē	Islands in the Pacific Ocean which are a state of the US (HI).
hawthorn	haw-thawn	
Hayes, Rutherford B	Hāz, Ruth-uh-fud Bē	19th president of the USA.
hay fever	hā fē-vuh	
hay wire	hā wī-uh	Out of order- to become crazy.
hazard	haz-ud	
hazardous	haz-ud-us	
head board	hed bō-ud	
header	hed-uh	
head gear	hed gē-uh	
head master	1) hed mas-tuh 2) hed mah-stuh	
head quarters	hed qwawt-uz	
head waters	hed wot-uz	
health care	helth kā-uh	
hear	hē-uh	

hearken	hah-kun	
heart	haht	
heart ache	haht āk	
heart breaker	haht brāk-uh	
heart failure	haht fā-ul-yuh	
heart warming	haht wom-in'	
heater	hēt-uh	
heather	he-"th"-uh	
heavenward	hev-un-wud	
heavy hearted	hevē haht-ed	
hectare	hek-tā-uh	A metric unit of measurement.
heifer	hef-uh	
heir	ā-uh	One who inherits.
Helena	Helen-uh	Capital of Montana.
helicopter	1) hel-uh-kop-tuh 2) hel-i-kop-tuh	
heliport	hel-uh-pō-ut	
hell	hel	Some believe, according to the Bible, hell is a place for bad people to go after death. Hell can also be an expression of exasperation. "Oh, hell!"
hello	hul-ō	Emphasis can be put on the "l" or the "o", depending on your mood when you greet someone.
hells-bells	helz-belz	An expression used when something unusual and surprising has happened that's beyond your control. "Well, hells-bells." It can mean, "Do you believe that!?" or "Oh my gosh, what's next?!" or any similar occasion.

helter skelter	hel-tuh skel-tuh	Chaos.
hemisphere	hem-is-fē-uh	
hemorrhage	hem-rij	
hemorrhoid	hem-rōyd	
hence forth	hens fō-uth	
heparin	hep-rin	
herald	hār-uld	
herb	urb	The "h" is silent.
herbalist	urb-ul-ist	
herbivore	erb-uh-vō-uh	
here	hē-uh	
hereafter	hē-uh-ahf-tuh	
here's	hē-uz	
here-to-fore	hē-uh-tōō-fō-uh	
heroin	hār-ō-in	
heron	hār-un	Long-legged bird that wades around the shoreline.
herring	hār-in'	
hexameter	hex-am-et-uh	
hibernate	hī-buh-nāt	
hide	hīd	WDE: hawīd
high born	hī bawn	
high chair	hī chā-uh	
higher up	hī-uh up	
high lighter	hī līt-uh	

high pressure	hī presh-uh	
high roller	hī rōl-uh	
high tide	hī tīd	WDE: hawī tawīd
high wire	hī wī-uh	
hinder	hind-uh	
hind quarter	hīnd qwaw-tuh	
hire	hī-uh	
hireling	hī-uh-lin'	
history	1) his-tuh-rē 2) hist-rē	
hither	hi-"th"-uh	
hither to	hi-"th"-uh tōo	Up until this time.
hoard	hō-ud	
hoar frost	hō-uh frawst	
hoarse	hō-us	
hobby horse	hob-ē hos	
hold over	hold ōvuh	
holier-than-thou	hōl-ē-uh-"th"an-"th"ow	A self-righteous attitude.
holler	hawl-uh	Yell, shout.
holograph	hawl-ō-grahf	
holographic	hawl-ō-grahf-ik	
holster	hōl-stuh	

Holy Roman
  Empire
	Hōl-ē Rōm-un
	  Em-pī-uh	

home care	hōm kā-uh	
home maker	hōm māk-uh	

home ward	hōm wud	
honey mooner	hunē mōōn-uh	
honor	awn-uh	
hookah	hook-uh	A pipe with a tube for drawing the smoke through a vessel of water, to cool it.
hooker (slang)	hook-uh	Prostitute.
Hoover, Herbert Clark	Hōōv-uh, Herb-ut Klahk	31st president of the USA.
hopper	hop-uh	
hormone	haw-mōn	
horn	hawn	
horned lizard	hawned liz-ud	
hornet	hawn-it	
horn pipe	hawn pīp	
horny	hawn-ē	1) Tough, calloused. 2) (slang) Sexually aroused.
horror	haw-ruh	
hors d'oeure	1) or durv 2) aw derv	
horse	hos	
horse feathers (slang)	hos fe-"th"-uz	Nonsense.
horse power	hos pow-uh	
horse's ass	hos-ez ahs	A person who's unlikeable due to offensive or inappropriate behavior – they can actually be repulsive.
horse sense	hos sens	Good common sense.
hortatory	haw-tuh-tor-ē	
horticulture	haw-ti-kul-chuh	

hot air	hot ā-uh	Useless talk.
hot potato	hot puh-tā-tō	A sexy, hot-blooded female.
hot tempered	hot tem-pud	
hour	ow-uh	
hour glass	ow-uh glahs	
house keeper	hows kēp-uh	
House of Lords	Hows ov Lauds	The uppuh house of the lej-i-slā-chuh of Great Britain.
house wares	hows wā-uz	
house warming	hows wawm-in'	
howitzer	how-its-uh	Short cannon, firing shells at a high trajectory.
howler	howl-uh	
how-so-ever	how-sō-ev-uh	
huckster	huk-stuh	A peddler.
humdinger	hum-ding-uh	Something very special in an exciting way.
humidor	hyōōm-uh-dō-uh	
humor	hyōō-muh	
humorous	hyōō-muh-rus	
hung over	hung ōv-uh	Feeling ill from having had too much of an alcoholic beverage.
hunker	hunk-uh	Usually used with the word "down" – to hunker down – to crouch or squat.
hydrocarbon	hī-drō-kah-bun	
hydrometer	hī-drawm-et-uh	
hydrosphere	hī-drō-sfē-uh	

hyper	hī-puh
hyperactive	hī-puh-ak-tiv
hysterectomy	his-tuh-rek-tum-ē

Ninth letter of the English Alphabet I,i (ī, awī)

Word	Pronunciation Examples	Notes
icebreaker	īs brāk-uh	
Idaho	Ī-duh-hō	Mountainous state in the NW USA. (ID) Capital: Boise.
identify	ī-den-ti-fī	WDE: awī-den-ti-fawī
ignore	ig-nō-uh	
ill flavored	il fā-vud	
ignorant	ig-nuh-runt	
ignore	ig-nō-uh	
Illinois	Il-uh-nō-ē	Midwest state of the US. (IL) Capital: Springfield.
illiterate	ilit-uh-rit	
ill mannered	il man-ud	
ill starred	il stahd	
ill tempered	il temp-ud	
imagine	im-aj-un	Many times, you'll also hear "magine", where the "i" is left off, altogether.
imagining	im-aj-in-in'	The "g" is often dropped on any word ending in "ing". It may be left in place when one wants to make more of a point – more emphasis.
immature	im-uh-chōō-uh	
immoderate	im-od-uh-rit	

immortal	im-aw-tul	
immortalize	im-aw-tul-īz	
immure	im-yōō-uh	To confine.
impair	im-pā-uh	
impairment	im-pā-uh-munt	
impala	im-pah-luh	Some may also say im-pal-uh, especially when referring to the make of the car, the Chevy Impala.
impale	im-pā-ul	
impart	im-paht	
impartial	im-pah-shul	
impassable	im-pahs-uh-bul	
impasse	im-pahs	
imperturbable	im-puh-turb-uh-bul	
implore	im-plō-uh	
imply	im-plī	WDE: im-plawī
import	im-pō-ut	
important	im-paw-tunt	
importunate	im-paw-chun-it	Persisting in asking or demanding.
imposing	im-pōz-in'	
imposter	im-pos-tuh	
imposture	im-pos-chuh	
impoverish	im-pawv-rish	
improper	im-prawp-uh	
improving	im-prōōv-in'	
impure	im-pyōō-uh	

impurity	im-pyur-uh-tē	
inaccurate	in-ak-yuh-rit	A note about "in" plus a root word. The "in" mostly implies "lack of" the root word.
inappropriate	in-uh-prō-prē-it	
incorrect	in-kaw-rekt	
incurable	1) in-kyur-uh-bul 2) in-kyōōr-uh-bul	
inseparable	in-sep-uh-ruh-bul	
inarticulate	in-ah-tik-yōō-lit	
inaugural	in-awg-yuh-rul	
inboard	in-bō-ud	
inborn	in-bawn	
inbreeding	in-brēd-in'	
incarcerate	in-kah-suh-rāt	
incarnadine	in-kah-nuh-dīn	To make red.
incarnate	in-kah-nit	
incinerate	in-sin-uh-rāt	
incline	in-klīn	WDE: in-klawīn
inconsiderable	in-kun-sid-uh-ruh-bul	
inconsiderate	in-kun-sid-uh-rit	
incorporate	in-kaw-puh-rāt	
incorrigible	in-kaw-rij-uh-bul	
incorruptible	in-kaw-rupt-uh-bul	
incubator	ink-yōō-bā-tuh	
incumber	in-kum-buh	

incur	in-kur	
indecipherable	in-de-sīf-uh-ruh-bul	
Indiana	In-dē-an-uh	Midwestern state in the USA. (IN). Capital: Indianapolis.
Indian corn	In-dē-un kawn	
Indian summer	In-dē-un sum-uh	An unusually warm spell in mid-October.
India paper	In-dē-ah pāp-uh	
indoor	in-dō-uh	
indorse	1) in-daws 2) in-dō-us	
industrial arts	in-dust-rē-ul ahts	
industrial park	in-dust-rē-ul pahk	
infarct	in-fahkt	
inferior	in-fēr-ē-uh	
inform	in-fawm	
informant	in-fawm-unt	
information	in-faw-mā-shun	
informative	in-fawm-uh-tiv	
informed	in-fawmd	
informer	in-fawm-uh	
inhaler	in-hāl-uh	
injure	in-juh	
innards	in-udz	
inner	in-uh	
inner ear	in-uh ē-uh	
inning	in-in'	

inn keeper	in kēp-uh	
inordinate	in-awd-in-it	
inorganic	in-aw-gan-ik	
inquire	in-kwī-uh	
insectivore	in-sekt-uh-vō-uh	
insecure	in-suh-kyo͞o-uh	
inshore	in-shō-uh	Near or toward the shore.
inside	in-sīd	WDE: in-sawīd
insider	in-sīd-uh	
insincere	in-sin-sē-uh	
in-so-far	in-sō-fah	
inspector	in-spekt-uh	
inspire	in-spī-uh	
instigator	in-stuh-gā-tuh	
instructor	in-strukt-uh	
insubordinate	in-suh-bawd-in-it	
insufferable	in-suf-uh-ruh-bul	
insular	in-suh-luh	1) Of or like an island. 2) Narrow-minded.
insuperable	in-so͞o-puh-ruh-bul	Can't be overcome.
insupportable	in-suh-pō-ut-uh-bul	
insure	1) in-sho͞o-uh 2) in-shō-uh	
insured	1) in-sho͞o-ud 2) in-shō-ud	
integer	in-tuh-juh	A whole number.
intellectual	in-tuh-lek-sho͞o-ul	

interact	1) in-ter-akt	
	2) in-tuh-act	
interactive	in-tuh-akt-iv	
interbreed	in-tuh-brēd	
intercourse	in-tuh-kō-us	
interdepartmental	in-tuh-dē-paht-ment-ul	
interfere	in-tuh-fē-uh	
interior	in-tēr-ē-uh	
interlard	in-tuh-lahd	To diversify.
interloper	in-tuh-lōp-uh	
interment	in-ter-munt	
interpersonal	in-tuh-pur-sun-ul	
interpose	in-tuh-pōz	
interracial	in-tuh-rā-shul	
interrupt	in-tuh-rupt	
intersection	in-tuh-sek-shun	
interstellar	in-tuh-stel-uh	
intertwine	in-tuh-twīn	WDE: in-tuh-twawīn
interview	in-tuh-vyōō	
inutero	in-yōō-tuh-rō	
investor	in-vest-uh	
investiture	1) in-vest-uh-chur	
	2) in-ves-uh-chōō-uh	
invigorate	in-vig-uh-rāt	
inward	in-wud	
inwardly	in-wud-lē	

in your face	in yaw fās	Someone is in your space, unwelcomed
ionosphere	ī-on-us-fē-uh	
iota	ī-ōtuh	An amount so small, it's next to nothing.
Iowa	Ī-ō-wuh	Midwestern state of the US. (IA)
IRA	Ī Ah Ā	A personal retirement plan – also the Irish Republican Army.
ire	ī-uh	Anger.
Ireland	Ī-uh-land	One of the British Isles west of Great Britain.
iron	ī-un	
iron ware	ī-un wā-uh	
irregardless	ēr-ē-gahd-les	There was a great man, singer, musician, and artist from Millbridge, ME who frequently used the term "irregardless" but modified it by adding a word in the middle to create his own "irrefuckin'gardless". Thank you, Nathan Hall. Sometimes it just fits the bill. May you RIP.
irregular	ēr-eg-yōō-luh	
irreverence	ēr-ev-runs	
irrevocable	ēr-ē-vōk-uh-bul	
irrupt	uh-rupt	
Ishtar	Ish-tah	A goddess of fertility for the people of ancient Babylon and Assyria.
isinglass	ī-zin-glahs	
islander	ī-lund-uh	A person born or living on an island.
isobar	ī-sō-bah	
isomer	ī-suh-muh	
iterate	it-uh-rāt	
itinerant	ī-tin-uh-runt	

itinerary	ī-tin-uh-rār-rē	
ivory tower	īv-rē tow-uh	

Tenth letter of the English Alphabet J,j (jā)

Word	Pronunciation Examples	Notes
jabber	jab-uh	
jack hammer	jak ham-uh	
jack-o-lantern	jak-uh-lan-tun	
Jackson, Andrew	Jak-sun, Andrōō	7th president of the USA.
jacquard	jak-ahd	A fabric with a figured weave.
jail	jā-ul	
jailer	jā-ul-uh	
janitor	1) jan-uh-tuh 2) jan-i-tuh	
January	Jan-yōō-ār-ē	First calendar month.
jar	jah	
jardinière	jah-duh-nēr	A pot or stand for plants or flowers.
jargon	jah-gun	
jasper	jas-puh	
jaw breaker	jaw brāk-uh	
jeer	jē-uh	
Jefferson, Thomas	Jef-uh-sun, Tom-us	3rd president of the USA.
Jefferson City	Jef-uh-sun Sit-ē	Capital of Missouri.
Jehovah	Juh-hō-vuh	Name of Almighty God of Christianity.
jeopardize	jep-ud-īz	

jeopardy	jep-uh-dē	
jerk warter	jerk waw-tuh	Not important, insignificant.
jester	jest-uh	
Jesus Christ	Jēz-us Krī-st	Son of the Almighty God and founder of Christianity.
jet port	jet pō-ut	
jewel	jōō-ul	
jeweler	1) jōō-ul-uh 2) jōōl-uh	
jewelry	1) jōō-ul-rē 2) jōōl-rē	
jews-harp	jōōz-hahp	Small musical instrument.
jigger	jig-uh	A small glass, usually of 1.5 ounces (measures liquor).
jitter bug	jit-uh bug	A fast dance for couples in the forties or fifties.
jitters	jit-uz	
jive	jīv	It is a fast dance for couples, similar to the jitter bug.
jive talk	jīv tok	When one is able to talk the common language of the younger folks – that is usually the teen years and into the early twenties.
jobber	job-uh	Wholesaler or does piece work.
jocular	jawk-yōō-luh	Full of fun.
jodhpurs	jawd-puz	Pants made for English style horseback riding.
jogging	jawg-in'	
Johnson, Andrew	Jon-sun, Andrōō	17th president of the USA.
Johnson, Lyndon Baines	Jon-son, Lin-don Bāns	36th president of the USA.

Word	Pronunciation	Notes
John the Baptist	No change.	He is in the Holy Bible. Some people call him John the Baptizer. He baptized many people, including Jesus.
joiner	jōēn-uh	
joker	jōk-uh	
juggernaut	jug-uh-nawt	
jugular	jug-yo͞o-luh	
jugular vein	jug-yo͞o-luh vān	
juicer	jo͞os-uh	
jumper	jump-uh	
jump start	jump staht	
Juneau	Jo͞on-ō	Capital of Alaska.
junior	jo͞on-yuh	
juniper	jo͞o-ni-puh	
junker	junk-uh	
Jupiter	Jo͞o-pi-tuh	Largest planet of our solar system.
juror	jur-uh	

Eleventh letter of the English Alphabet K,k (kā)

Word	Pronunciation Examples	Notes
K	Kā	1) In baseball, a K stands for a strike out. 2) Karat (or carat) – weight of precious gemstones such as diamonds. 3) A thousand dollars. 4) Symbol for potassium. 5) Symbol for kilometer.
kale	kā-ul	A type of cabbage.
kangaroo court	kang-guh-ro͞o cō-ut	

Kansas	Kan-zus	Midwestern state in USA. (KS) Capital: Topeka.
kaput	kah-put	Done, gone, destroyed.
karma	kahm-uh	Fate, sort of.
kart (cart)	kaht	
kayak	kī-ak	
keel	kē-ul	The bottom of a boat- that's why to "keel over" literally means to capsize but can mean someone fell over or even died.
keeper	kēp-uh	
Kennebec	Ken-ē-bek	A county in Maine.
Kentucky	Ken-tuk-ē	A state in the USA with many, many horses! (KY) Capital: Frankfort.
kerosene	kār-uh-sēn	
ketar (katar)	kuh-tah	Old-fashioned word used when referring to the phlegm that would accumulate in a person's throat overnight, then raised up and expectorated on awakening – occurs more often in the elderly.
Kevlar	Kev-lah	Trademark used for the material in bulletproof vests.
key board	kē bō-ud	
Key West	Kē West	An island (part of Florida) in the Gulf of Mexico.
khaki	kah-kē	A tan color. Some people say ka-kē – but not a Mainer.
kibitzer	kib-itz-uh	A schmoozer/meddler.
kick start	kik staht	
kife (slang)	kīf	Stealing very sneakily – usually not caught.
killer	kil-uh	
killer bee	kil-uh bē	
killer whale	kil-uh wā-ul	

kiloliter	kil-uh-lē-tuh	
kilometer	1) kil-om-eh-tuh 2) kil-ō-mē-tuh	
kilter	kil-tuh	In good order – the opposite of "out of kilter".
kindergarten	1) kin-dē-gah-den 2) kin-duh-gah-den	
kind hearted	kīnd haht-ed	
king fisher	kēng fish-uh	
King Lear	Kēng Lē-ah	Chief character in one of Shakespeare's plays.
kipper	kip-uh	
kitchen ware	kich-en wā-uh	
kitty cornered	kit-ē kawn-ud	At an angle.
klutz	kluhtz	About the same as a gawm.
kneeler	nē-ul-uh	
knickers	nik-uz	
knit ware	nit wā-uh	
knocker	nok-uh	
Knox	Nawx	A county in Maine.
knuckle head	nuk-ul hed	A bozo – someone who's not too sharp.

Twelfth letter of the English Alphabet L,l (el)

Word	Pronunciation Examples	Notes
L	el	Roman numeral for 50.
labor	lā-buh	
laborer	lā-buh-ruh	

Labrador retriever	Lab-ruh-dō-uh rē-trēv-uh	These are great dogs who usually love water. Their coat is short and thick/dense and water repellant.
lacerate	las-uh-rāt	
lackluster	lak-lust-uh	
lacquer	lak-uh	
ladder	lad-uh	
lady finger	lā-dē fing-guh	
lady slipper	lā-dē slip-uh	A lovely, delicate type of orchid that grows often in secluded areas, like woods. Also called lady's slipper and may be white or pinkish.
lager	lah-guh	
laggered	lag-ud	Slow- someone who doesn't keep up with the others.
lair	lā-uh	
lassez faire	lā-zā fā-uh	A French word - freedom of control by someone.
lambaste	lam-bāst	To really let someone "have it", physically or verbally, usually surprising to the recipient.
lancer	lan-suh	A soldier with a lance.
landholder	land hōld-uh	
landing gear	landin' gē-uh	
land lord	land lawd	
land lubber	land lub-uh	One with little experience with sailing or out on the water, in general.
land mark	land mahk	
landward	land-wud	Forward land.

languor	lang-guh	Similar to being languid – weak, listless.
lantern	lan-tun	
lanyard	lan-yud	
lap board	lap bō-ud	
lar board	lah bud	Port (left) side of the boat.
larceny	lah-sen-ē	
larch	lah-ch	A tree of the pine family.
lard	lahd	
larder	lahd-uh	Pantry.
large	lahj	
large hearted	lahj hahted	
largo	lah-gō	Slow, stately music.
lark	lahk	
larva	lah-vuh	
lazer	lā-zuh	
lass	lahs	A good young woman.
lassie	lahs-ē	Affectionate term for a good young woman or girl.
lasso	1) lah-sō 2) lah-sō͞o	
last	lahst	
lather	la-"th"-uh	
latter	lat-uh	
laugh	lahf	
laughter	lahf-tuh	
launder	lawn-duh	

lavalier	lah-vuh-lē-uh	A chain worn around the neck, usually with an ornament on it.
lavender	lav-en-duh	
law breaker	law brāk-uh	
law giver	law giv-uh	
law maker	law māk-uh	
lawn mower	lawn mō-uh	
lawyer	law-yuh	
layer	lā-uh	
lay over	lā ōv-uh	
leader	lēd-uh	
leap year	lēp yē-uh	Every fourth year when February has one <u>more</u> day, so it's 29 instead of 28.
leather	le-"th"-uh	
leather neck	le-"th"-uh nek	A US Marine.
lecher	lech-uh	
ledger	lej-uh	
leer	lē-uh	
leeward	lē-wud	Away from the wind.
Leeward Islands	Lē-wud Ī-lundz	Part of the West Indies.
left over	left ō-vuh	
legal tender	lē-gul ten-duh	
legerdemain	lej-uh-duh-mān	Sleight of hand.
leg horn	leg hawn	
Legislature	Lej-uh-slā-chuh	
leisurely	le-"zh"-uh-lē	

lemur	lē-muh
leopard	lep-ud
leotard	lē-uh-tahd
leper	lep-uh
lessor	les-uh
lethargy	leth-uh-jē
letter	let-uh
letter carrier	let-uh kār-ē-uh
lever	lev-uh
liar	lī-uh
liberal	lib-rul
liberal arts	lib-rul ahts
libertarian	lib-uh-tār-ē-un
libertine	lib-uh-tēn
liberty	lib-uh-tē
licorice	1) lik-rish 2) lik-aw-rish
lie	lī WDE: lawī
lie detector	lī dē-tek-tuh
lieutenant general	lōō-ten-unt jen-rul
lieutenant governor	lōō-ten-unt guv-uh-nuh
life form	līf fawm
life guard	līf gahd
life preserver	līf prez-urv-uh
life raft	līf rahft

life support	līf suh-pō-ut	
ligature	lig-uh-chōō-uh	
lighter	līt-uh	
light fingered	līt fing-gud	
light hearted	līt haht-ed	
light opera	līt op-ruh	
light year	līt yē-uh	
like minded	līk mīn-did	WDE: līk mawīn-did
lily livered	lilē liv-ud	
limber	lim-buh	
limburger cheese	lim-burg-uh chēz	
limerick	lim-rik	
Lincoln, Abraham	Link-un, Ābruh-ham	16th president of the USA.
Lincoln	Link-un	1) County in Main. 2) Capital of Nebraska.
linear	lin-ē-uh	
line backer	līn bak-uh	
liner	līn-uh	
linger	ling-guh	
lion hearted	lī-un hahted	
liquor	lik-uh	
liter	lē-tuh	
literature	lit-ur-uh-chōō-uh	
lithium carbonate	lith-ē-um kah-bun-it	
lithograph	1) lith-uh-grahf 2) lith-ō-grahf	

lithosphere	lith-uh-sfē-uh	
litter	lit-uh	
litter bug	lit-uh bug	Highly disliked in Maine.
Little Dipper	Lit-ul Dip-uh	A group of stars shaped like an old fashioned soup or water dipper – also contains the North Star.
Little Rock	Lit-ul Rawk	Capital of Arkansas.
live bearer	līv bār-uh	
liver	liv-uh	
livery	liv-rē	
lizard	liz-ud	
load star	lōd stah	
loafer	lōf-uh	
loaner	lōn-uh	
loan shark	lōn shahk	
lobster	lob-stuh	Maine is known for this delicious shellfish and the sturdy fishermen that catch them.
lobster tail	lob-stuh tā-ul	
locker	lok-uh	
lode star	lōd stah	
lodger	loj-uh	
logger	log-uh	
loiter	lōē-tuh	
loner	lōn-uh	
long hair	long hā-uh	
Long Island	Long Ī-lund	In Southeast New York – a distinctive accent of their own.

long shoreman	long shō-uh-mun	
looker on	look-uh on	An observer.
looking glass	lookin' glahs	
lord	lawd	
Lord's Day	Lawdz Dā	
lordship	lawd-ship	
Lord's Prayer	Lawdz Prā-uh	Matthew 6:9-13 – Starts with "Our Father"…
lore	lō-uh	
lorry	law-rē	
lottery	lawt-uh-rē	
loudspeaker	lowd-spēk-uh	
louie (slang)	lōō-ē	Expectorated sputum.
Louisiana	Lōō-ēz-ē-an-uh	Southern state of the USA on the Gulf of Mexico. (LA) Capital: Baton Rouge.
lounge wear	lownj wā-uh	
love	luv	
love affair	luv uh-fā-uh	
love lorn	luv lawn	Very sad because of being in love with someone who doesn't love them.
lover	luv-uh	
low born	lō bawn	
lower	lō-uh	
lower classman	lō-uh klahs-mun	

Word	Pronunciation	Notes
low-tide	lō-tīd	WDE: lō-tawīd – The tide on the east coast of the US flows in and out on a regular schedule. Low tide is when the water has drawn furthest away from the land. The water will flow back into the land and reach the uppermost point, called high tide. It takes <u>about</u> six hours for the tide to go out- then <u>about</u> six ours to flow back in.
Lucifer	L$\overline{oo}$-suf-uh	Another name for the devil.
lukewarm	l$\overline{oo}$k-wawm	
lumbar	lum-bah	
lumber	lum-buh	
lumber jack	lumbuh jak	
lumberman	lumb-uh-mun	
lunar	l$\overline{oo}$n-ah	To do with the moon.
lure	l$\overline{oo}$-uh	To attract or entice.
luster	lus-tuh	
lyre	lī-uh	A small type of harp.

Thirteenth letter of the English Alphabet M,m (em)

Word	Pronunciation Examples	Notes
macabre	1) muh-kahb 2) muh-kahb-ruh	
Mach number	Mahk num-buh	Has to do with speed of sound.
macerate	mas-uh-rāt	
machinery	muh-shēn-rē	
mackerel	mak-rul	
madder	mad-uh	

made-to-order	mād-tōō-awd-uh	
Madison, James	Mad-uh-sun, Jāmz	4rth president of the USA.
Madison	Mad-uh-sun	Capital of Wisconsin.
'magine	maj-in	Short for imagine – used often in Maine.
Magna Carta	Mag-nuh Kah-tuh	The charter granted in 1215 that guarantees certain civil and political liberties to the English people.
magnetic field	mag-net-ik fē-uld	
magnetometer	mag-nuh-tom-uh-tuh	
maharajah	mah-huh-rah-juh	
maiden hair	mād-en hā-uh	
maid of honor	mād ov awn-uh	
mail carrier	mā-ul kār-ē-uh	
mail order	mā-ul awd-uh	
Maine	Mān	Northern-most New England state of the USA. (ME)
Mainer	Mān-uh	One who is from or lives in Maine.
main mast	1) mān mahst 2) mān mast	
main sail	mān suhl	Principle and largest sail on the main mast.
maître d'	mā-truh dē	
major	mā-juh	
make over	māk ō-vuh	
malaria	muh-lar-ē-uh	
malarkey	muh-lahk-ē	Foolish talk – usually not true.
malefactor	mal-eh-fakt-uh	Someone who does bad or illegal things.

malformation	mal-fawm-ā-shun	
malinger	muh-ling-guh	
malingerer	muh-ling-guh-ruh	
mallard	mal-ud	A wild duck. The male is beautifully colored – female is a shade of brown.
malt liquor	mawlt lik-uh	
mama or mamma	1) mah-muh 2) mum-uh	See also mum or mum-uh. They are all words a child uses for his/her mother.
managed care	man-ijd kā-uh	
manager	man-ij-uh	
man eater	man ēt-uh	
maneuver	muh-nōō-vuh	
manger	mān-juh	
man hour	man-ow-uh	
manicure	man-uh-kyōō-uh	
Manila paper	Muh-nil-uh pāp-uh	
manner	man-uh	
mannered	man-ud	
mannerism	man-uh-rizm	
mannerly	man-uh-lē	
man of letters	man ov let-uz	One in the field of literature.
man of war	man ov waw	
manometer	mun-om-eh-tuh	
manor	man-uh	
manpower	man-pow-uh	
mansard	man-sahd	A type of roof.

manslaughter	man-slaw-tuh	
manure	muh-noo-uh	
mar	mah	
maraca	1) muh-rahk-uh 2) muh-rah-kuh	
marble	mah-bul	
marbled	mah-buld	
march	mahch	
March	Mahch	3rd month of the year.
march hare	mahch hā-uh	A sort of rabbit ready for breeding – an example of madness.
marching orders	mahchin' awduz	
Mardi Gras	Mah-dē Grah	Last day before Lent – a great party in New Orleans.
mare	mā-uh	Female horse.
mare's nest	mā-uz nest	A hoax or a mess.
margarine	mah-juh-rin	
margin	mah-jin	
marginal	mah-jin-ul	
mariachi	mar-ē-ah-chē	
marijuana	mār-uh-wawn-uh	A hemp plant smoked for enjoyment.
mark	mahk	
marina	muh-rēn-uh	
marine	muh-rēn	To do with the sea.
Marine Corps	Muh-rēn Kō-uh	A proud branch of the armed forces of the USA – trained to fight on land, at sea, and in the air.

mariner	mār-in-uh	
marjoram	mah-juh-rum	
mark	mahk	
marked	mahkt	
market	mah-ket	
market share	mahket shā-uh	
marksman	mahks-mun	
mark up	mahk up	
marlin	mah-lin	Large deep sea fish.
marmalade	mah-muh-lād	
marmoset	1) mah-mō-set 2) mah-muh-set	
marmot	mah-mut	Thick-bodied rodents.
marque	mahk	
marquise	mah-kē	
Mars	Mahz	1) Planet of our solar system. 2) A Roman god of War.
marsh	mah-sh	
marshal	mah-shul	
marshmallow	1) mahsh-mulō 2) mahsh-melō	
marsupial	mah-sōōp-ē-ul	A mother mammal that carries her young in a pouch over her abdomen.
mart	maht	
marten	mah-tun	
martial	mah-shul	
martial arts	mah-shul ahts	

Martian	Mah-shun	A being from Mars.
martin	mah-tin	A type of bird.
martini	mah-tē-nē	
martyr	mah-tuh	
marvel	mah-vul	
marvelous	mah-vul-us	
Maryland	Mār-uh-lund	State of the East USA. (MD)
marzipan	mah-zi-pan	
mask	1) mahsk 2) mask	
Massachusetts	Mas-uh-chōō-sets	New England State in the USA. Go Boston! Boston Strong! Capital: Boston.
massacre	mas-uh-kuh	
masseur	muh-sōō-uh	
mast	1) mahst 2) mast	
master	mas-tuh	
Master of Arts	Mas-tuh ov Ahts	
masturbate	mas-tuh-bāt	
matador	mat-uh-dō-uh	
matriarch	mā-trē-ahk	
matron of honor	mā-trun ov awn-uh	
matter	mat-uh	
mature	1) muh-chōō-uh 2) muh-tōō-uh	
maunder	mawn-duh	Confused action.

maverick	mav-rik	
may flower	mā flow-uh	
mayor	mā-uh	
mayoral	mā-aw-rul	
mazel tov	mah-zul-tof	
McKinley, William	Mik-in-lē Wil-yum	25th president of the USA.
meager	mē-guh	
meal	mē-ul	
mealy mouthed	mēlē mou-"th"-ed	
meander	mē-and-uh	
measure	me-"zh"-uh	
measured	me-"zh"-ud	
Medicaid	Med-i-kād	Financial assistance for health care
Medicare	Med-i-kā-uh	provided by the state and federal government.
mediocre	mēd-ē-ōk-uh	
Mediterranean	Med-uh-ter-ān-ē-un	Sea and surrounding area.
member	mem-buh	
memoirs	mem-wahz	
mental retardation	mentul rē-tahd-ā-shun	
mentor	men-tō-uh	
mere	mē-uh	
merely	mē-uh-lē	
merge	merj	
merger	merj-uh	
mesmerize	mez-muh-rīz	

messenger	mes-en-juh	
metacarpus	met-uh-kah-pus	
metamorphosis	met-uh-maw-fuh-sis	
metaphor	met-uh-fō-uh	
metatarsus	met-uh-tah-sus	
meteor	mē-tē-ō-uh	
meter	mē-tuh	
metre	mē-tuh	English way of writing meter.
mettle	met-ul	
mew	mē-o͞o	
mezzosoprano	mezō-suh-prah-nō	
Michigan	Mish-uh-gun	Midwestern state of the USA. (MI) Capital: Lansing.
micro computer	mīkrō kum-pyo͞o-tuh	
micrometer	1) mīkrō-mē-tuh 2) mī-krawm-uh-tuh	
microprocessor	mīkrō-praw-ses-uh	
mid air	mid ā-uh	
mid course	mid kō-us	
middle class	midul klahs	
middle ear	midul ē-uh	
minge	minjē	A tiny flighty, biting insect – even smaller than a black fly. Some people call them "No See Ums".
midsummer	mid-sum-uh	
midwinter	mid-win-tuh	
midyear	mid-yē-uh	

mild	mī-uld	
mile	mī-ul	
mileage	mīl-ij	
miler	mī-ul-uh	
milliliter	mil-uh-lē-tuh	
millimeter	mil-uh-mē-tuh	
milliner	mil-in-uh	
millionaire	mil-yun-ā-uh	
mimeograph	mim-ē-ō-grahf	
mind	mīnd	
mind reader	mīnd rēd-uh	
miner	mīn-uh	
mineral water	1) min-uh-rul waw-tuh 2) min-rul waw-tuh	
miniature	min-uh-chōō-uh	
minicomputer	minē-kum-pyōō-tuh	
minister	min-is-tuh	
Minnesota	Min-uh-sō-tuh	Midwestern state of the USA. (MN) Capital: Saint Paul.
minor	mī-nuh	
miniscule	min-is-kyōō-ul	Very small, maybe as tiny as a minge.
mire	mī-uh	
mirror	mēr-uh	
misdemeanor	mis-duh-mēn-uh	A minor offense under law.
miser	mī-zuh	
misfire	mis-fī-uh	

misfortune	mis-faw-chōͦn	
misgovern	mis-guv-un	
mishear	mis-hē-uh	
misinform	mis-in-fawm	
misnomer	mis-nō-muh	
Mississippi	Mis-is-ip-ē	Southern state of the USA. (MS) (Also a long, large river in center US.) Capital: Jackson.
Missouri	1) Muh-zoō-rē 2) Muh-zur-ē	Midwest state of the USA. (MO) Capital: Jefferson City.
mister	mis-tuh	
mistletoe	mis-ul-tō	An evergreen with shiny green leaves and white berries. Around Christmas time, people make a simulation with red berries. Often, people will kiss under mistletoe during the Christmas and New Years holidays.
misunderstand	mis-unduh-stand	
miter	mīt-uh	
mixed number	mikst num-buh	
mixer	miks-uh	
mixture	miks-chuh	
mizzen mast	miz-en mahst	
mobster	mob-stuh	
mockery	mok-uh-rē	
moderate	mod-uh-rit	
moderator	mod-uh-rāt-uh	
modern	mod-un	
modernism	mod-un-izm	

modular	mod-jōō-luh	
moire	mwah	
moisture	mō-ēs-chuh	
Mojave Desert	Mō-hah-vē Dez-ut	In Southeast California.
molar	mōl-uh	
molasses	muh-lahs-ez	
molder	mōl-duh	
monarch	mon-ahk	
monarchist	mon-ahk-ist	
moneymaker	munē māk-uh	
money market	munē mah-ket	
money order	munē awd-uh	
moniker	mawn-ik-uh	
monitor	mawn-uh-tuh	
monk	munk	
monkey	munk-ē	
Monroe, James	Munrō, Jāmz	5th president of the USA.
monster	mawn-stuh	
Montana	Mawn-tan-uh	Mountain state of the NW USA. (MT) Capital: Helena.
Monte Carlo	Mawn-tē Kah-lō	A gambling resort in Monaco.
Montgomery	Mont-gum-rē	Capital of Alabama.
Monticello	Mawnti-selō	Home and burial place of Thomas Jefferson in VA.
Montpelier	Mawnt-pēl-yuh	Capital of Vermont.

mooring	mō-uh-rin'	Where the boat is tied up out on the water when not in use.
moored	mō-ud	Being tied at the mooring.
moral	maw-rul	
morale	mawr-al	
moralize	maur-ul-īz	
morbid	maw-bid	
more	mō-uh	
more over	mō-uh ōv-uh	
morgue	maw-g	
Mormon	Maw-mun	Member of the church of Jesus Christ of Latter Day Saints, founded in 1830 in the USA.
Morn	Mawn	
morning	mawn-in'	
moron	1) mō-uh-ron 2) mawr-on	
morose	mawr-ōs	
morphine	maw-fēn	
mortal	maw-tul	
mortality	maw-tal-uh-tē	
mortar	mawt-uh	
mortar board	maw-tuh bō-ud	
Moses	Mōz-ez	The leader in the Bible who brought the Israelites out of Egypt (and slavery) and gave them laws from Almighty God.
mosquito	muh-skē-tō	
motor	mō-tuh	

motor car	mō-tuh kah	
mountaineer	mown-tun-ē-uh	
Mouseketeer	Mows-kuh-tē-uh	A member of the children's group in the 1950s who belonged to the Mikey Mouse Club – sponsored by Walt Disney and continues today.
mover	mo͞ov-uh	
mover and shaker	mo͞ov-uh and shāk-uh	A sort of business person who deals in a number of business opportunities and takes chances to make money. Often moves quickly from one venture to another.
muffler	muf-uh-luh	1) A scarf worn around one's throat to keep warm. 2) A device where all the exhaust from the car goes to deaden noise and cut back on emissions.
mug	muhg	1) (slang) For someone's face. 2) A sort of cup to hold coffee or other beverage.
mugger (slang)	mug-uh	Term for someone who assaults a person, usually to rob them.
muleteer	myo͞ol-uh-tē-uh	One who drives mules and skins mules.
multimillionaire	multē-mil-ē-un-ā-uh	
multiprocessor	multē-praw-ses-uh	
mum	No change.	1) Short for chrysanthemum. 2) Quiet, not talking. 3) What you call your mother in place of mom.
mummer	mum-uh	
murder	mur-duh	
murderer	mur-duh-ruh	
Muscatel	Mus-kuh-tel	Sweet wine from the muscat grape.
muscular	mus-kyo͞o-luh	
musketeer	mus-kuh-tē-uh	A soldier who carried a musket (gun).

mustard	mus-tud	
mustard gas	mus-tud gas	Named for its mustard-like odor – very damaging to anyone in contact.
muster	mus-tuh	
mutter	mut-uh	
Mylar	Mī-lah	
mystery	1) mist-rē 2) mist-er-ē	
mythology	mith-ol-uh-jē	

Fourteenth letter of the English Alphabet N,n (en)

Word	Pronunciation Examples	Notes
nabob	nā-bob	Rich or important man.
nacre	nā-kuh	Mother of pearl.
nadir	nā-duh	Lowest point.
nail	nā-ul	
nail biter	nā-ul bīt-uh	
narc	nahk	A law enforcer dealing with narcotics.
narcissism	nah-sis-izm	
narcosis	nah-kō-sis	
narcotic	nah-kot-ik	
narcotize	nah-kuh-tīz	
narwhal	nah-wā-ul	Small whale – lives in the Arctic.
NASCAR	Nas-kah	National Association for Stock Car Auto Racing.

Nashville	Nash-vil	Capital of Tennessee. Also is the world headquarters for country music
National Guard	Nash-un-ul Gahd	
native born	nātiv bawn	
natural	nach-rul	
naturally	nach-rul-ē	
natural resource	nach-rul rē-sō-us	
nature	nā-chuh	
naughty	nawt-ē	Bad or improper, disobedient behavior.
nausea	naw-shuh	Urge to vomit.
nautical mile	naw-tik-ul mī-ul	A unit of measure used in navigation – equal to 1.1508 land miles.
Navajo	Nah-vuh-hō	Native American tribe of people of SW USA, also spelled Navaho.
navigator	nav-uh-gā-tuh	
nay sayer	nā sā-uh	Habitually denies or refuses.
Neanderthal	Nē-and-uh-thawl	
neap tide	nēp tīd	Either of the two lowest tides in the month.
near	nē-uh	
nearby	nē-uh-bī	
nearly	nē-uh-lē	
Nebraska	Nuh-brahs-kuh	Midwestern state of the USA. (NE) Capital: Lincoln.
neckerchief	nek-uh-chif	
neck wear	nek wā-uh	
nectar	nek-tuh	

nectarine	nek-tah-rēn	
nefarious	nuh-fāh-rē-us	Very wicked.
neighbor	nā-buh	
neither	1) nē-"th"-uh 2) nī-"th"-uh	
nephew	nef-yōō	
nerve center	nerv sen-tuh	
nether	ne-"th"-uh	Lower or under.
Netherlands	Ne-"th"-uh-lundz	In West Europe.
neuromuscular	nerō-musk-yōō-luh	
neuter	nōō-tuh	
Nevada	Nuh-vah-duh	Mountain state of the Western USA. (NE) Capital: Carson City.
never	nev-uh	
never more	nev-uh mō-uh	
never the less	nev-uh "th"-uh les	
new born	nōō bawn	
new comer	nōō cum-uh	
New England	Nōō Ing-lund	Six US states in New England: ME, VT, NH, MA, RI, and CT.
New Englander	Nōō Ing-lund-uh	One who lives in or is from New England.
New Jersey	Nōō Jerz-ē	Northeastern state of the USA. (NJ) Capital: Trenton.
New Mexico	Nōō Mex-i-kō	Southern state of the USA. (NM) Capital: Santa Fe.
news caster	nōōz kast-uh	

news paper	nōōz pāp-uh	
New Testament	Nōō Testuh-munt	Second part of the Holy Bible – the Greek Scriptures.
New Years	Nōō Yē-uz	
New York	Nōō Yawk	Northeastern state of the USA. (NY) Capital: Albany.
next door	neks dō-uh	
nicker	nik-uh	A soft neigh – a sound a horse makes.
nicotine	nik-uh-tēn	
niggard	nig-ud	Stingy, miserly person.
night crawler	nīt krawl-uh	
nightmare	nīt mā-uh	
night wear	nīt wā-uh	
nincompoop	nin-kum-pōōp	A stupid, aggravating person.
nipper	nip-uh	
Nixon, Richard Millhouse	Nix-un, Rich-ud Mil-hows	37th president of the USA.
no brainer	nō brān-uh	
noir	nwah	French for "black", but is used in English to describe a book or movie with a prevailing dark mood.
nomenclature	nawm-en-klā-chuh	
nonabsorbent	non-ab-saw-bunt	
non-allergenic	non-al-uh-jen-ik	
nonbeliever	non-bē-lēv-uh	
nonbellilgerent	non-buh-lij-uh-runt	
non-chargeable	non-chahj-uh-bul	

nonconforming	non-kun-fawm-in'
non-corroding	non-kuh-rōd-in'
noncorrosive	non-kuh-rō-siv
non-departmental	non-dē-paht-ment-ul
nondrinker	non-drink-uh
non-enforceable	non-enfō-us-uh-bul
non-granular	non-gran-yōō-luh
nonhazardous	non-haz-ud-us
nonhereditary	non-hered-uh-tār-ē
noninterference	non-in-tuh-fēr-ens
nonliterary	non-lit-uh-rār-rē
nonmember	non-mem-buh
nonnarcotic	non-nah-kot-ik
nonoperational	non-op-uh-rā-shun-ul
nonpaying	non-pā-in'
non-recoverable	non-rē-kuv-uh-ruh-bul
nonrecurring	non-rē-kur-in'
nonresistant	non-rēz-ist-unt
non-secular	non-sek-yōō-luh
nonsmoker	non-smō-kuh
nonspeaking	non-spēk-in'
non-specializing	non-speshal-īz-in'
non-staining	non-stān-in'
nonstandard	non-stan-dud
non-sticking	non-stik-in'

non-striking	non-strīk-in'	
non-supporting	non-su-pō-ut-in'	
non-thinking	non-think-in'	
non-uniform	non-yōōn-uh-fawm	
nonuser	non-yōōz-uh	
nonvoter	non-vōt-uh	
nonconductor	non-kun-dukt-uh	
nonconformist	non-kun-fawm-ist	
nonintervention	non-in-tuh-ven-chun	
nonpartisan	non-paht-is-un	
nonsectarian	non-sek-tār-ē-un	
nonsupport	non-suh-pō-ut	
no-no (slang)	nō-nō	Something you shouldn't do.
nor	Naw	
Nordik	Naw-dik	
Nor Easter	Naw Ēst-uh	Severe storm with the wind blowing toward the North East.
norm	nawm	
normal	naw-mul	
Norse	Naws	Scandinavian.
north	nawth	
North Carolina	Nawth Kār-ō-līn-uh	South East state of the USA. (NC) Capital: Raleigh.
North Dakota	Nawth Duh-kō-tuh	Midwestern state of the USA. (ND) Capital: Bismark.
northeastward	nawth-ēst-wud	

northerly	naw-"th"-uh-lē	
northerner	naw-"th"-un-uh	
Northern Ireland	Naw-"th"-un Īr-lund	This division of the United Kingdom is the North East part of the island of Ireland.
Northern Lights	Naw-"th"-un Līts	Also called Aurora Borealis.
North Star	Nawth Stah	
northward	nawth-wud	
norwester	naw-west-uh	A wild storm with the wind blowing in from the North West.
nose guard	nōz gahd	
November	Nō-vem-buh	
nowadays	now-uh-dāz	Means in the current times – unlike "back in the day" refers to a past time period.
nowhere	nō-wā-uh	
nuclear	nōō-klē-uh	
number	num-buh	
numerator	nōōm-uh-rā-tuh	
nurture	nurch-uh	
nut cracker	nut krak-uh	

Fifteenth letter of the English Alphabet O,o (ōh)

Word	Pronunciation Examples	Notes
O	Ō	The character that stands for zero, a blood type, and is the chemical symbol for oxygen.
Oahu	Ō-ah-ho͞o	The main island of Hawaii.
oar	ō-uh	One of the paddles that sit in the oar locks in order to row a small boat.
oar lock	ō-uh lok	Holds the oar in place.
obdurate	1) ob-duh-rit 2) ob-duh-rāt	Stubborn.
obelisk	ob-ul-isk	
objurgate	ob-juh-gāt	Rebuke.
obliterate	ō-blit-uh-rāt	Devastate.
obscure	ob-sko͞o-uh	Faint, vague.
observation	ob-suh-vā-shun	
obstreperous	ob-strep-uh-rus	
oceanography	ō-shun-og-ruh-fē	
ocher	ōk-uh	
October	Awk-tō-buh	10th month of the year.
ocular	awk-yo͞o-luh	To do with the eyes.
OD	Ō-dē	1) Slang for an overdose. (ō-vuh-dōs) 2) Also stands for right eye (ocular dexter).
odd ball (slang)	awd bawl	Unusual or eccentric person.
odds maker	awdz māk-uh	
odometer	ō-dawm-etuh	

161

odor	ō-duh	
odiferous	ō-dif-uh-rus	
o'er	ō-uh	Short for over.
off color	awf kul-uh	
offer	awf-uh	
office holder	awf-is hōl-duh	
officer	awf-is-uh	
off shore	awf shō-uh	
off year	awf yē-uh	
ogre	ō-guh	
Ohio	Ō-hī-ō	Midwestern state of the USA. (OH) Capital: Columbus.
ohm meter	ōm mē-tuh	
oil color	ō-ē-ul kul-uh	
Oklahoma	Ōk-luh-hōm-uh	Sate of the USA. (OK) Capital: Oklahoma City.
okra	ōk-ruh	
Oktoberfest	Awk-tō-buh-fest	A German beer-drinking festival held in Germany and elsewhere.
old bat (slang)	ōld bat	A derogatory name for cranky, mean "old" women.
older	ōld-uh	
Old Glory	1) Ōld Glō-rē 2) Ōld Glaw-rē	Nickname for the flag of the USA – the stars and stripes.
old guard	ōld gahd	
old master	1) ōld mast-uh 2) ōld mahst-uh	

Old Norse	Ōld Naws	
oldster	ōld-stuh	
old timer	ōld tīm-uh	Usually wise older person.
Old Testament	Ōld Test-uh-munt	The first part of the Holy Bible made up of Hebrew scriptures.
oleander	ō-lē-and-uh	
oleomargarine	ō-lē-ō-mah-juh-rin	
oligarchy	awlig-ahkē	A ruling few in the government.
omnipotent	awm-ni-puh-tent	All powerful.
omnivorous	awm-niv-aw-rus	Eats any sort of food.
once over	wuns ōv-uh	
on looker	awn look-uh	
onward	awn-wud	
onyx	awn-iks	
open air	ō-pun ā-uh	
open hearted	ō-pun haht-ed	
open hearth	ō-pun hahth	
opera	awp-ruh	
operate	awp-uh-rāt	
operation	awp-uh-rā-shun	
operator	awp-uh-rā-tuh	
operetta	awp-uh-ret-uh	
ophthalmology	awp-thuh-mawl-uh-jē	
opportunity	awp-uh-tōōn-uh-tē	
opposite	1) awp-sit 2) awp-uh-sit	

opposite number	awp-sit num-buh	
opposition	awp-uh-zi-shun	
oppression	1) aw-presh-un 2) ō-presh-un	
oracle	awr-uh-kul	
oral	aw-rul	
oratory	aw-ruh-tōr-ē	
orb	awb	
orbit	1) awb-it 2) aw-bit	
orchard	aw-chud	
orchestra	1) aw-kis-truh 2) aw-kes-truh	
orchid	aw-kid	
ordain	aw-dān	
ordeal	aw-dē-ul	
order	awd-uh	
orderly	aw-duh-lē	
ordinance	aw-dun-uns	
ordinary	aw-dun-ār-ē	
ordure	aw-jur	Filth.
ore	ō-uh	
oregano	awr-eg-un-ō	
Oregon	Awr-uh-gawn	A Northwestern state in the USA. (OR) Capital: Salem.
organ	aw-gun	
organdy	aw-gun-dē	

organic	aw-gan-ik	
organism	1) aw-gan-izm 2) aw-gun-izm	
organist	1) aw-gan-ist 2) aw-gun-ist	
organize	aw-gun-īz	
organza	aw-gan-zuh	Thin fabric of silk, rayon, etc – has a stiff feeling.
orgasm	aw-gaz-um	
orgy	aw-jē	
orient	aw-rē-ent	
Oriental	Aw-rē-ent-ul	
orifice	aw-ruh-fīs	
origami	aw-ri-gahm-ē	
origin	awr-uh-jin	
original	1) awr-ij-un-ul 2) ō-rij-un-ul	
oriole	aw-rē-ōl	
ormolu	aw-mul-ōō	Imitation gold.
ornament	awn-uh-munt	
ornate	aw-nāt	
ornery	awn-uh-rē	Mean, stubborn.
ornithology	aw-rinth-awl-uh-jē	The study of birds.
orphan	aw-fun	
Orpheus	Aw-fē-us	Mythical being with magical, musical powers.
ortho	aw-thō	

orthodox	aw-thō-doks	Conforming to conventional beliefs.
orthography	aw-thawg-ru-fē	All about spelling correctly! What a joke! This book would be very confusing for an orthographist.
orthopedics	aw-thō-pēd-iks	
osteoarthritis	awst-ē-ō-ahth-rī-tis	
other	uh-"th"-uh	
otherwise	uh-"th"-uh-wīz	
otter	1) awt-tuh 2) aw-tuh	An animal with webbed feet, is furry, and loves water.
our	1) ow-uh 2) ah	
ours	ow-uz	
ourselves	ow-uh-selvz	
ouster	ow-stuh	
out board	out bō-ud	
out door	out dō-uh	
out doors	out dō-uz	Some people say "out of doors".
outer	out-uh	
outer space	out-uh spās	
outerwear	out-uh-wā-uh	
outlast	out-lahst	
out maneuver	out mun-ōō-vuh	
out number	out num-buh	
out-of-doors	out-ov-dō-uz	
out-of-towner	out-of-town-uh	
outrider	out-rīd-uh	

out rigger	out rig-uh	
outside	out-sīd	WDE: out-sawīd
out sider	out sīd-uh	
out smart	out smaht	
out ward	out wud	
over	ō-vuh	
overeager	ō-vuh-ē-guh	
over exercise	ō-vuh eks-uh-sīz	
over generous	1) ō-vuh jen-rus 2) ō-vuh jen-uh-rus	
over tire	ō-vuh tī-uh	
over bearing	ō-vuh bār-in'	
over board	ō-vuh bō-ud	
over charge	ō-vuh chahj	
over here	ō-vuh hē-uh	
overlord	ō-vuh-lawd	
over master	1) ō-vuh mahs-tuh 2) o-vuh mas-tuh	
overpower	ō-vuh-pow-uh	
over the counter	ō-vuh "th"-uh kown-tuh	
overture	ō-vuh-chōō-uh	
Oxford	Awks-fud	County in Maine.
oyster	ō-ē-stuh	
ozone layer	ō-zōn lā-uh	

Sixteenth letter of the English Alphabet P,p (pē)

Word	Pronunciation Examples	Notes
pace maker	pās māk-uh	
pacifier	pas-uh-fī-uh	
package store	pak-ij stō-uh	
pager	pāj-uh	
pain killer	pān kil-uh	
painter	pān-tuh	
painting	1) pān-tin' 2) pānt-in'	
pair	pā-uh	
palaver	puh-lav-uh	Idlesome talk.
pale	pā-ul	
pall bearer	pawl bār-uh	
pallor	pal-uh	
Palm Sunday	1) Pahm Sun-dā 2) Pahm Sun-dē	The Sunday before Easter (the resurrection of Jesus) when he entered Jerusalem and palms were strewn before him.
palomino	pal-uh-mē-nō	A tan or blonde horse with a white mane and tail.
pamper	pam-puh	
pander	pan-duh	
panhandler	pan-hand-luh	
pannier	pan-ē-uh	Large basket to carry items on the back.
panorama	pan-uh-rah-muh	
panther	pan-thuh	

paper	pā-puh	
paper hanger	pā-puh hang-uh	
paper trail	pā-puh trā-ul	
par	pah	
para (a prefix)	pār-uh	Beside, beyond, or helping.
paragraph	pār-uh-grahf	
parallel parking	pār-uh-lel pah-kin'	
parameter	pah-ram-et-uh	
paramour	pāruh-mōō-uh	
paraphernalia	pār-uh-fuh-nāl-yuh	
parboil	pah-bō-ē-ul	
parcel	pah-sul	
parch	pah-ch	
parchment	pahch-munt	
pardon	pah-dun	
pare	pā-uh	
paregoric	pār-uh-gaw-rik	
par excellence	pah eks-uh-lahns	
parfait	pah-fā	
pariah	puh-rī-uh	An outcast.
parishioner	puh-rish-un-uh	A member of the parish (or church).
park	pahk	
parka	pahk-uh	
parking meter	pahk-in' mēt-uh	
Parkinson's Disease	Pah-kin-sunz Dis-ēz	

park way	pahk wā	
parlance	pah luns	Way of speaking.
parlay	pah-lā	Staking one's winnings to gamble for more.
parley	pah-lē	Conference to settle a dispute.
parliament	pah-li-ment	
parlor	pah-luh	
parmesan	pah-muh-"zh"-on	Cheese type.
parquet	pah-kā	Type of flooring.
parse	pahs	
parsimony	pah-suh-mō´-nē	Very frugal.
parsley	pah-slē	
parsnip	pah-snip	
parson	pah-sun	
parsonage	pah-sun-ij	
part	paht	
partake	pah-tāk	
parted	paht-ed	
parterre	pah-tuh	A flower garden in a pattern.
parthenogenesis	pah-then-ō-jen-uh-sis	Reproduction without fertilization.
Parthenon	Pah-thuh-non	
partial	pah-shul	
participate	pah-tis-uh-pāt	
participle	pah-tis-uh-pul	
particle	pah-tik-ul	

particolored	pah-tē-kul-ud	
particular	pah-tik-yōō-luh	
particulate	1) pah-tik-yōō-lāt 2) pah-tik-yōō-lit	
parting	paht-in'	
partisan	pah-tis-un	
partition	pah-ti-shun	
partly	paht-lē	
partner	paht-nuh	
part of speech	paht ov spēch	
partook	pah-took	
partridge	pah-trij	
part song	paht song	
part time	paht tīm	WDE: paht tawīm
part timer	paht tīm-uh	WDE: paht tawīm-uh
part way	paht wā	
party	paht-ē	
party goer	paht-ē gō-uh	
pass	1) pahs 2) pas	
passable	pahs-uh-bul	
passage	1) pah-sij 2) pas-ij	
passageway	1) pah-sij wā 2) pas-ij wā	
pass book	1) pahs book 2) pas book	

passé	pah-sā	French- old fashioned gone by.
passel	pas-ul	Large group.
passenger	pahs-en-juh	
passer by	pahs-uh-bī	
passers by	pahs-uz bī	
pass-fail	pahs-fā-ul	
passing	1) pahs-in' 2) pas-in'	
passion	pash-un	
passionate	pash-un-it	
passive	1) pahs-iv 2) pas-iv	
passive-aggressive	pahs-iv/uh-gres-iv	
passive-resistance	pahs-iv/rez-ist-uns	
pass key	1) pahs kē 2) pas-kē	
Passover	Pahs-ōv-uh	Ancient Jewish holiday to commemorate freeing the Hebrews from slavery to the Egyptians. The pharaoh decided to let the Hebrews go after Jehovah sent the angel of death to kill all the firstborn sons of the Egyptians. Pharaoh's firstborn son was included in those who were killed. After all the previous plagues, that was the "final straw". Pharaoh ordered the Hebrews be allowed to leave Egypt. You see, the angel of death didn't kill any of the firstborn sons of the Hebrews. The angel "passed over" the homes of the Hebrews. Therefore, it is called "Passover".
passport	1) pahs-pō-ut 2) pas-pō-ut	

password	pahs-werd	
past	Pahst	
pasta	pahst-uh	
paste	pāst	
pasteboard	pāst-bō-ud	
pastel	past-el	Soft, light colors.
pastern	pas-turn	Part of a horse's hoof – just above the hoof.
pasteurize	pahs-chur-īz	
pastime	pahs-tīm	Spending spare time.
pastor	pas-tuh	In charge of a religious congregation.
pastoral	pas-taw-rul	
pastrami	puh-strah-mē	
pasture	pahs-chuh	
patent leather	pat-ent le-"th"-uh	
Pater Noster	Pateh Nawst-uh	The Lord's Prayer in Latin.
path	1) pahth 2) path	
pathetic	puh-thet-ik	
patina	puh-tē-nuh	
patriot	pā-trē-ut	One who loves and supports their country.
petrol car	puh-trōl kah	
patter	pat-uh	
pattern	pat-un	
Paul Bunyan	Pawl Bun-yun	From American folklore — a giant lumberjack who had a giant blue ox named "Babe". They performed superhuman feats.

173

pauper	paw-puh	
pawn broker	pawn brōk-uh	
paymaster	1) pā-mast-uh 2) pā-mah-stuh	
peacemaker	pēs-māk-uh	
peace officer	1) pēs of-uh-suh 2) pēs of-i-suh	
peal	pē-ul	
Peanut Gallery	Pē-nut Gal-uh-rē	The term was invented by Buffalo Bob on the Howdy Doddy Show back in the early 1950s. It caught on as a popular term for any group of children gathered together for the purpose of observing/responding.
pear	pā-uh	
Pearl Harbor	Purl Hah-buh	Inlet on the South coast of Oahu, Hawaii. This is the site of the Japanese bombing on Dec. 7th, 1941 – The entry of the US onto WWII.
packing order	pa-kin' awd-uh	
peculiar	1) puh-kyōōl-yuh 2) pē-kyool-yuh	
pedicure	pedi-kyōō-uh	
pedometer	ped-om-i-tuh	
peer	pē-uh	1) An equal 2) Looking closer, trying to see better.
Pegasus	Peg-uh-sis	A mythical winged horse.
peg board	peg-bō-ud	
pelagic	pul-aj-ik	Just a nice word meaning the ocean or open sea – beautiful – rhymes with magic.
pelf	No change.	Money or wealth regarded with contempt.

pell-mell	No change.	To be in a jumble, or a wild, disorderly haste.
Penn, William	Pen, Wil-ē-um	1844-1718, an English Quaker and founder of Pennsylvania.
Pennsylvania	Pen-sil-vān-ē-uh	State in the North East US. (PA) Capital: Harrisburg.
penny pincher	pen-ē pinch-uh	A miser/tight-wad.
Penobscot	1) Pen-ob-skot 2) Puh-nob-skot	A county in Maine. Also where Bangor (Bang-gaw) is. The Penobscot river flows between Bangor and Brewer on its way to the ocean (at Bucksport - Buks-pōut).
pentagon	pen-tuh-gawn	A figure with five angles and five sides. The US Defense Department has an office building that's pentagonal, near Washington DC.
Pentateuch	Pen-tuh-took	The first five books of the Bible.
pepper corn	pep-uh kawn	Dried berry of the pepper.
pepper shaker	pep-uh shāk-uh	
perambulator	1) pur-am-byo͞o-lāt-uh 2) pur-am-byo͞o-lā-tuh	A baby carriage.
percolator	1) pur-kō-lāt-uh 2) pur-ko-lā-tuh	
peregrine	pār-eh-grin	A swift falcon.
perform	1) puh-fawm 2) per-fawm	To do, to fulfill, to render, to enact.
perfumery	per-fyo͞om-uh-rē	Many perfumes.
perhaps	pur-haps	
pericardium	1) pār-e-kahd-ē-um 2) pār-uh-kahd-ē-um	The thin, closed sack that surrounds the heart.
perimeter	puh-rim-eh-tuh	The outer boundary.

peripheral	puh-rif-uh-rul	
perjure	pur-juh	Gave false witness under oath.
perpendicular	pur-pun-dik-yo͞o-lah	
persevere	pur-suh-vē-uh	Persist even if hard to do.
perspire	pur-spī-uh	Sweat.
pervert	1) puh-vert 2) pur-vert	One who practices perversion.
pester	pes-tuh	
petard	puh-tahd	A kind of firecracker.
peter	pē-tuh	Dwindle until gone.
petro dollars	pe-trō dawl-uz	Money from the sale of oil.
pettifogger	pe-tē-fawg-uh	A lawyer with poor ethics and petty cases.
petty officer	pe-ti awf-is-uh	A naval noncommissioned officer.
pewter	py o͞o-tuh	
phalange	1) ful-anj-ē 2) fuh-lanj-ē	
pharmaceutical	fahm-uh-s o͞o-ti-kul	
pharmacist	fahm-uh-sist	
pharmacy	fahm-uh-sē	
phenobarbital	fēn-ō-bahb-i-tawl	
philander	fil-and-uh	Engages lightly in love affairs.
philharmonic	fil-hah-maw-nik	
philter/philtre	fil-tuh	A magic potion or charm.
phone card	fōn cahd	
phonograph	fō-nō-grahf	
phosphor	faws-fuh	A fluorescent substance.

photograph	fō-tō-grahf	
pickerel	1) pik-uh-rul 2) pik-rul	Fierce freshwater fish of the pike family.
picture	pik-chuh	
picture window	pik-chuh win-dō	
pie chart	pī chaht	
pier	pē-uh	
pierce	1) pē-us 2) pērs	
piker (slang)	pīk-uh	One who does things in a petty or stingy way.
pilchard	pil-chud	
pile driver	pī-ul drī-vuh	
pillar	pil-uh	
pinafore	pin-uh-fō-uh	
pine	pīn	WDE: pawīn
pine tar	pīn tah	
pinfeather	pin-fe-"th"-uh	
pin setter	pin set-uh	Someone or something that resets the bowling pins up.
pioneer	pī-un-ē-uh	
pipe fitter	pīp fit-uh	
pipe organ	pīp aw-gun	
pismire	1) pis-mī-uh 2) pis-uh-mī-uh	An ant.
Piscataquis	Pis-cat-uh-qwis	A county in Maine.
pitch dark	pich dahk	
pitcher	pich-uh	

pitter patter	pit-uh pat-uh	Tapping sounds occurring in rapid succession, such as a hard rain storm.
pit viper	pit vī-puh	
placard	plak-ud	
placer	plās-uh	
plantar	plan-tah	To do with the sole of the foot.
planter	plan-tuh	Holds plants for growing.
plaster	plahs-tuh	
plaster board	plahs-tuh bō-ud	
plate glass	plāt glahs	
platform	plat-fawm	
platter	plat-uh	
player	plā-uh	
play goer	plā gō-uh	
playing cards	plā-in' kahds	
plaza	plah-zah	
plea-bargain	plē-bah-gin	
pleasure	ple-"zh"-uh	
pliers	plī-uz	
plover	pluv-uh	
plow share	plow shā-uh	
plumber	plum-uh	
plumber's helper	plum-uhz help-uh	
plunder	1) plund-uh 2) plun-duh	
Plymouth	Plim-uth	A town in Southeast Massachusetts, settled by Pilgrims in 1620.

pockmark	pawk-mahk	A scar left because of a pustule from smallpox or severe acne.
pointer	pō-ēn-tuh	
poker	pōk-uh	
poker face	pōk-uh fās	A face with little or no expressions (so to not give the hand away).
polar	pōl-ah	
polar bears	pōl-ah bā-uz	A large, white ferocious bear, along the coastal arctic areas.
polarize	pōl-uh-rīz	
Polaroid	Pōl-uh-rō-ēd	Now an old fashioned camera, but still produces pictures in seconds.
pole star	pōl stah	Polaris, the North Star.
police officer	puh-lēs off-is-uh	Just one of the many in the police force.
policy holder	pol-is-ē hold-uh	
politically correct	pō-lit-ik-al-ē kaw-rekt	
Polk, James K.	Pōk, Jāmz Kā	11th president of the US.
pollster	pōl-stuh	
poltergeist	pōl-tuh-gīst	
polyester	pawlē-est-uh	
polygraph	pawlē-grahf	
polymer	1) pawl-ē-muh 2) pawl-uh-muh	
pompadour	pom-puh-dō-uh	A hairdo where the hair is brushed up high from the forehead.
ponder	pawn-duh	
ponderous	pawn-duh-rus	
poniard	pawn-yud	A dagger.

poor	pō-uh	
poorhouse	pō-uh hows	An institution for people down on their luck.
popcorn	pop-kawn	
poplar	pop-luh	Tall tree of the willow family.
popover	pop-ōvuh	A light, puffed up, hollow muffin. The Jordan Pond house, by Acadia National Park in Seal Harbor, ME was famous for their afternoon homemade popovers and tea.
popular	pop-yōō-luh	
porcelain	pō-uh-suh-lin	
porch	pō-uch	
porcine	pō-uh-sēn	A type of pig or hog.
porcupine	1) paw-kyōō-pīn 2) paw-kē-pīn	
pore	pō-uh	
pork	pō-uk	
porky	pō-ukē	
porn	1) pawn 2) pō-un	
pornography	1) pawn-og-ruh-fē 2) pō-un-og-ruh-fē	
porpoise	pawp-us	
porringer	paw-rinj-uh	A shallow bowl.
port	pō-ut	
portable	1) pō-ut-uh-bul 2) pawt-uh-bul	
portage	pō-ut-ij	
portend	paw-tend	

portent	1) pō-ut-ent	
	2) paw-tent	
portentous	paw-ten-chus	
porter	1) pō-ut-uh	
	2) pawt-uh	
porterhouse	1) paw-tuh-hows	A type of horse or steak.
	2) pō-ut-uh-hows	
portfolio	pō-ut-fōl-ē-ō	
porthole	pō-ut-hōl	
portico	1) pō-uh-tik-ō	
	2) paw-ti-cō	
portion	1) pō-uh-shun	
	2) paw-shun	
Portland	Pō-ut-lund	1) A city in NW Oregon. 2) A city in southern coastal Maine - one of the more active ME cities.
portly	pō-ut-lē	
portrait	1) paw-trit	
	2) pō-uh-trit	
portray	pō-uh-trā	
portulaca	1) paw-chōō-lak-uh	Fleshy plants with yellow, pink, or purple flowers.
	2) paw-chuh-lahk-uh	
poser	pōz-uh	
posse	paw-sē	
possess	1) pō-zes	
	2) puh-zes	
postcard	pōst-kahd	
poster	pōst-uh	
post mark	pōst mahk	

post master	1) pōst mahs-tuh 2) pōst mas-tuh	
post modernism	pōst maw-dun-izm	
post mortem	pōst maw-tum	After death.
post partum	pōst pah-tum	After childbirth.
post war	pōst waw	
pot boiler	pawt bō-ē-ul-uh	
potholder	pawt-hōld-uh	
potter	pawt-uh	
potter's field	potuz fē-uld	
potter's wheel	potuz wē-ul	
pour	pō-uh	Fluid to flow out freely.
poverty	paw-vuh-tē	
powder	pow-duh	
power	pow-uh	
practitioner	prak-tish-un-uh	
prairie schooner	prār-ē skōōn-uh	Large covered wagon.
prayer	prā-uh	
preacher	prēch-uh	
preceptor	prē-sep-tuh	
precursor	prē-kur-suh	
predecessor	pred-uh-ses-uh	
prefigure	prē-fig-yuh	
premature	prē-muh-chōō-uh	
premiere	1)prem-ē-uh 2)pruh-me-uh	

preordain	prē-aw-dān	
prepare	prē-pā-uh	
prerecord	prē-rē-kawd	
presbyter	prez-bi-tuh	A priest or elder in some churches.
present participle	prez-unt pah-tis-uh-pul	
preserve	prez-urv	
pressure	presh-uh	
pressure cooker	presh-uh kook-uh	
prevailing	prē-vā-ul-in'	
prewar	prē-waw	
prier	prī-uh	
primer	prīm-uh	
primogeniture	prē-mō-jen-i-tuh	The exclusive right the eldest son has to an inheritance.
primordial	prīm-awd-ē-ul	
prince consort	prins kon-sawt	Husband for a reigning queen.
principle parts	prin-suh-pul pahts	
prior	prī-uh	
prisoner	1) priz-un-uh 2) priz-uh-nuh	
privateer	prī-vuh-tē-uh	
probation officer	prō-bā-shun of-is-uh	
procedure	prō-sē-juh	
proctor	prawk-tuh	
procurator	prō-kyōouh-rā-tuh	

procure	prō-kyōō-uh	
procurer	prō-kyōōr-uh	
professor	1) pruh-fes-uh 2) prō-fes-uh	
proffer	1) prof-uh 2) praw-fuh	An offer of an intangible something, like friendship.
profiteer	praw-fuh-tē-uh	
progenitor	prō-jen-uh-tuh	
progesterone	prō-jest-uh-rōn	
projector	prō-jekt-uh	
promoter	prō-mō-tuh	
prong horn	prawng hawn	An animal resembling the deer and antelope but has curved horns.
propeller	prō-pel-uh	
proper	praw-puh	
property	praw-puh-tē	
proportion	prō-pō-uh-shun	
proprietor	prō-prī-uh-tuh	
prospector	praws-pect-uh	
prosper	praws-puh	
protector	prō-tekt-uh	
protractor	prō-trakt-uh	
provender	prō-vend-uh	
provider	prō-vīd-uh	
provost guard	prō-vōst gahd	
puberty	pyōō-buh-tē	

public defender	pub-lik duh-fend-uh	
pucker	puk-uh	
puffer	puf-uh	
pullover	pul-ō-vuh	
pull motor	pul mō-tuh	
pulsar	pul-sah	
pumpernickel	pump-uh-nik-ul	
puncture	punk-chuh	
punster	pun-stuh	Someone who likes to make puns.
puppeteer	pup-uh-tē-uh	
pure	py$\overline{oo}$-uh	
purport	pur-pō-ut	
purser	purs-uh	
pusher	push-uh	
pushover	push-ō-vuh	
putter	put-uh	
pyre	pī-uh	

Seventeenth letter of the English Alphabet Q,q (ky $\overline{oo}$)

Word	Pronunciation Examples	Notes
QC (Quebec)	Qwi-bek	A province of Canada.
quadrennial	kwo-dren-ē-ul	
quagmire	kwag-mī-uh	
Quaker	Kwā-kuh	A member of the Society of Friends.

185

qualifier	kwal-uh-fī-uh	
qualm	kwawm	
quark	kwahk	Matter from outer space.
quart	kwawt	
quarter	kwaw-tuh	
quarter horse	kwaw-tuh hos	
quarter master	1) kwaw-tuh mahs-tuh 2) kwaw-tuh mas-tuh	
quartet	kwaw-tet	
quartz	kwawtz	Crystalline mineral.
quasar	kwā-zah	
quaver	kwā-vuh	
queer	kwē-uh	
question mark	kwest-jun mahk	
questionnaire	kwest-jun-ā-uh	
quick silver	kwik sil-vuh	
quick tempered	kwik temp-ud	
quipster	kwip-stuh	
quire	kwī-uh	
quitter	kwit-uh	
quiver	kwiv-uh	
quotation mark	kwō-tā-shun mahk	

Eighteenth letter of the English Alphabet R,r (ah)

Word	Pronunciation Examples	Notes
rabble rouser	rab-ul rowz-uh	
race horse	rās hos	
racing form	rās-in' fawm	
racketeer	raket-ē-uh	
raconteur	rak-un-tōō-uh	One skilled at telling stories.
radar	rā-dah	
radar scope	rā-dah skōp	
radial tire	rād-ē-ul tī-uh	
radiator	rā-dē-ā-tuh	
raft	rahft	
raider	rād-uh	
rain storm	rān stawm	
rain water	rān waw-tuh	
rambler	ram-bluh	
rampart	ram-paht	An defensive barrier, like a castle wall.
rancor	rank-aw	Ongoing ill will, even hate.
ranger	rān-juh	
rapier	rāp-ē-uh	A light, sharp-pointed sword.
rapper	rap-uh	
rapport	ruh-pō-uh	
raptor	rap-tuh	A bird that preys on animals.
rapture	rap-chuh	Overwhelmed with joy/love.

rasher	rash-uh	
rather	ra-"th"-uh	
rathskeller	rath-skel-uh	A restaurant below street level, usually, where beer is served.
rattler	rat-ul-uh	
raw bar	raw bah	
razor	rāz-uh	
razor wire	rāz-uh wī-uh	
reacquire	rē-uh-kwī-uh	
reappear	rē-uh-pē-uh	
rearm	rē-ahm	
reborn	rē-bawn	
recharge	rē-chah-j	
recover	rē- kuv-uh	
rediscover	rē-dis-cuv-uh	
reembark	rē-em-bahk	
reenter	rē-en-tuh	
rehear	rē-hē-uh	
rehire	rē-hī-uh	
renumber	rē-num-buh	
reorder	rē-awd-uh	
reupholster	rē-up-hōl-stuh	
reactor	rē-ak-tuh	
readership	rēd-uh-ship	
Reagan, Ronald Wilson	Rā-gun, Ron-uld Wil-sun	40th president of the USA.

realtor	rē-ul-tuh	
reamer	rēm-uh	
reaper	rēp-uh	
reapportion	rē-uh-pō-uh-shun	
rear	rē-uh	
rear admiral	rē-uh ad-muh-rul	
rearward	rē-uh-wud	
recapture	rē-cap-chuh	
receiver	rē-sēv-uh	
receptor	rē-sept-uh	
recliner	rē-klīn-uh	
reconnoiter	rē-kun-ō-ē-tuh	
reconsider	rē-kun-sid-uh	
record	1) rē-kawd 2) rek-ud	1) The act of recording. 2) The synthetic, thin disk that sound is recorded upon.
recording	rē-kawd-in'	
recourse	rē-kō-us	
recover	rē-kuv-uh	
rectilinear	rek-tuh-lin-ē-uh	Formed by straight lines.
rector	rek-tuh	A clergyman.
red carpet	red kah-pet	
red deer	red dē-uh	
red-letter	red-let-uh	
red snapper	red snap-uh	
red tide	red tīd	WDE: red tawīd

reefer (slang)	rēf-uh	Slang for marijuana cigarette.
reflector	rē-flek-tuh	
reform	rē-fawm	
reformatory	1) rē-fawm-uh-tōr-ē 2) rē-fawm-uh-taw-rē	
reformer	rē-fawm-uh	
refrigerator	rē-frij-uh-rā-tuh	
regale	rē-gā-ul	
regard	rē-gahd	
register	rej-ist-uh	
registered nurse	rej-is-tud nurs	RN. (Ah En)
registrar	rej-is-trah	
regular	reg-yōō-luh	
reincarnation	rē-in-kah-nā-shun	
reindeer	rān-dē-uh	
reinforce	rē-in-fō-us	
rejigger	rē-jig-uh	To alter the terms.
rejoinder	rē-jō-ēn-duh	
remainder	rē-mān-duh	
remark	rē-mahk	
remarkable	rē-mahk-uh-bul	
remember	rē-mem-buh	
remorse	rē-maws	
render	rend-uh	
reorganize	rē-awg-un-īz	

repair	rē-pā-uh
repairman	rē-pā-uh-mun
repartee	1) rē-pah-tā 2) rep-ah-tē
repertoire	rep-uh-tawh
report	rē-pō-ut
reporter	rē-pō-ut-uh
reptile	rep-tī-ul
require	rē-kwī-uh
reservoir	rez-uh-vwah
resister	rē-zist-uh
resonator	rez-un-ā-tuh
resort	1) rē-zawt 2) rez-awt
resource	rē-sō-us
resourceful	rē-sō-us-ful
respirator	res-puh-rā-tuh
restaurant	1) rest-rawnt 2) rest-runt
restore	1) rēs-tō-uh 2) rē-stō-uh
retainer	rē-tān-uh
retard	rē-tahd
retardant	rē-tah-duhnt
retarded	rē-tahd-ed
retire	ruh-tī-uh
retort	rē-tawt

retriever	rē-trēv-uh	
retro fire	retrō fī-uh	
revere	1) rēv-ē-uh 2) rē-vē-uh	
reverence	rev-rens	
reverend	rev-rend	
revile	rē-vī-ul	
Revolutionary War	Rev-uh-lōō-shun-ār-ē Waw	The American Revolution.
revolver	rē-vawl-vuh	
reward	rē-wawd	
RH factor	Ah-Āch fak-tuh	A factor in the blood of humans and the Rhesus monkey. Some people have it (RH+ positive) and some people don't (RH- negative).
Rhode Island	Rōd Ī-lund	A New England US state. (RI) Capital: Providence.
rhubarb	1) rōō-bub 2) rōō-bahb	
rhymer	rīm-uh	One who makes rhymes.
rider	rī-duh	
rigmarole	rig-uh-muh-rōl	This is how this word is pronounced in Maine.
rigor	rig-uh	
rigormortis	rig-uh-maw-tis	
rile	rī-ul	
ringer	ring-uh	
ring leader	ring lēd-uh	

ring master	1) ring mas-tuh 2) ring mahs-tuh	
Rio Grande	1) Rēo Grand 2) Rēo Grand-ē	
rip cord	rip cawd	
riser	rīz-uh	
rival	rī-vul	
river	riv-uh	
riverside	riv-uh-sīd	
road kill (slang)	No change.	A dead animal, usually living near the roadside or even in the road, that was killed by a passing vehicle. This is a very sad situation to most Mainers.
road side	rōd sīd	WDE: rōd sawīd. The area known as the berm.
roan	rōn	A color of a horse. It can be brown, black, or reddish BUT flecked with numerous white hairs. Roy Rogers once sang a great song called "Oh, That Strawberry Roan". Many others sang different versions of this amusing song.
rock bottom	rawk bawtum	Described in Websters as the "lowest level". However, Mainers have a saying about feeling "lower than whale shit". I believe they are about even.
rocker	rawk-uh	This can be something that rocks back and forth because of the curved pieces that support it OR it can be a person who plays rock and roll music.
rock garden	rawk gah-dun	
rocking horse	rawk-in' hos	
rodeo	1) rō-dē-ō 2) rō-dā-ō	
Roger	Raw-juh	Name of a signal flag. 1) Received. 2) OK!

roister	rō-ēs-tuh	Noisy and crazy partying.
roller	rōl-uh	
roller bearing	rōl-uh bār-in'	
roller blade	rōl-uh blād	
roller coaster	rōl-uh kōst-uh	
roller skate	rōl-uh skāt	
Roman Empire	Rō-mun Em-pī-uh	
romper	rawmp-uh	
roof	rōōf	Sometimes called "ruf", as in <u>foo</u>t.
roofer	rōōf-uh	
room and board	rōōm and bō-ud	
roomer	rōōm-uh	
Roosevelt, Franklin Delano	Rōz-uh-velt, Frank-lin Del-uh-nō	32nd president of the US.
Roosevelt, Theodore	Rōz-uh-velt Thē-uh-dō-uh	26th president of the US.
rooster	rōōs-tuh	
root beer	rōōt bē-uh	
Roque fort	Rōk fut	A type of cheese.
rose colored	rōs kul-ud	
rose water	rōs waw-tuh	
roster	ros-tuh	A list.
rot gut	rawt gut	A low-grade liquor.
rotor	rō-tuh	
round tripper (slang)	round trip-uh	A home run in baseball.
rubber	rub-uh	

rudder	rud-uh
ruler	rōōl-uh
rumor	rōōm-uh	Something that is talked about but probably not based on fact or first-hand knowledge.

run over	run ō-vuh
runner	run-uh
rupture	rup-chuh
rush hour	rush ow-uh
rustle	rus-ul

Nineteenth letter of the English Alphabet S,s (es)

Word	Pronunciation Examples	Notes
saber	sā-buh	
sabre saw	sā-buh saw	
sachet	sash-ā	
Sacramento	Sak-ruh-men-tō	Capital of California.
saddle	sad-ul	
saddle horse	sad-ul hos	
safari	suh-fah-rē	
safer	sāf-uh	
safe guard	sāf gahd	
safety glass	sāf-tē glahs	
safety razor	sāf-tē rā-zuh	
safflower	saf-flow-uh	
Sagadohoc	Sag-uh-duh-hawk	County in Maine.

Sagittarius	Saj-uh-tā-rē-us	Ninth sign of the Zodiac - a fire element sign.
sail	sā-ul	
sail board	sā-ul bō-ud	
sailor	sāl-uh	
Saint Patrick's Day	Sānt Pat-riks Dā	March 17th every year - the celebration of Saint Patrick, the patron saint of Ireland. He converted the pagans to Christians, and it is said that he drove all the snakes out of Ireland. This day is celebrated not just by the Irish, but also by the millions of people who are Irish at heart OR just love a great party. Great music.
Saint Valentine's Day	Sānt Val-en-tīnz Dā	February 14th of every year, there is a celebration in honor of the martyr of the third century. People express fondness and love for special people in their lives by giving candy (especially chocolates), flowers, cards, and phoning.
salaam	suh-lahm	A greeting in India and the near East. You would also bow to show respect when saying "suh-lahm".
salad bar	sal-ad bah	
salamander	sal-uh-mand-uh	
Salem	Sā-lum	Capital of Oregon – also, Salem, Massachusetts is famous for the witch trials in the early days of the country.
sale	sā-ul	
salary	sal-uh-rē	
salicylic acid	sal-uh-sil-ik as-id	Asprin.
salmon	sam-un	A fish that spawns in fresh water (returns to where it was born) and returns to the salt water where it lives.
salt cellar	sawlt sel-uh	Any salt holder or shaker.

Salt Lake City	Sawlt Lāk Sit-ē	Capital of Utah.
salt peter	sawlt pē-tuh	Said to deter sexual drive.
salt pork	sawlt pō-uk	
salt shaker	sawlt shāk-uh	
salt water	sawlt waw-tuh	Sea or ocean (except for the Great Salt Lake in the western US).
salve	sahv	(Not sav in Maine.)
sampler	samp-luh	
San Antonio	San An-tō-nē-ō	City in Texas, where the Alamo is.
sand bar	sand bah	
sand dollar	sand dol-uh	Flat, round creatures that live on the sandy ocean beds- can be found on the sandy beaches so well, especially at low tide.
sand paper	sand pā-puh	
sand piper	sand pī-puh	Small shore bird.
sand storm	sand stawm	
San Juan	San Wawn	Capital of Puerto Rico.
sans	sahnz	French for without.
Santa Fe	San-tuh Fā	Capital of New Mexico.
sapphire	saf-ī-uh	Precious deep blue clear stone.
sap sucker	sap suk-uh	An American woodpecker.
sarcasm	sah-kazm	Generally ironic remarks that have a tone of facetiousness.
sarcastic	sah-kast-ik	
sarcoma	sah-kōm-uh	Cancer of connective tissues.
sarcophagus	sah-kof-uh-gus	

sardine	sah-dēn	Edible, small ocean fish.
sardonic	sah-don-ik	Scornful.
sarsaparilla	sas-puh-ril-uh	
sartorial	sah-taw-rē-ul	Tailors or their work.
sass	sahs	To talk disrespectfully.
satire	sat-ī-uh	
satisfactory	sat-is-fakt-uh-rē	
Saturday	1) Sat-uh-dā 2) Sat-uh-dē	
Saturn	Sat-un	Second largest planet in the solar system.
saucer	saw-suh	
sauerbraten	sow-uh-brawt-en	
sauerkraut	sow-uh-krowt	
saunter	sawn-tuh	
savior	sāv-yuh	Jesus Christ (in Christianity).
savoire faire	sav-wah fā-uh	
savor	sāv-uh	
saw horse	saw hos	
sawyer	saw-yuh	
scabbard	skab-ud	Sheath for a blade.
scalawag	skal-ē-wag	A scamp or rascal.
scale	skā-ul	
scallop	skawl-up	This is one of the most mispronounced of all the sea foods. So many people say "skallup". It is so wrong.
scamper	skamp-uh	

scar	skah	
scarce	skā-us	Hard to find.
scare	skā-uh	
scarf	skahf	
scarlet	skah-let	
scarlet fever	skah-let fē-vuh	
scatter	skat-uh	
scatterbrain	skat-uh brān	Poor concentration.
scavenger	skav-enj-uh	
scenery	1) sēn-rē 2) sēn-uh-rē	
scepter	sep-tuh	
schnauzer	shnowz-uh	A sturdy, active dog with a wiry coat - of the terrier family.
scholar	skawl-uh	
school board	skōōl bō-ud	
school marm	skōōl mahm	
school master	1) skōōl mahs-tuh 2) skōōl mast-uh	
school teacher	skōōl tēch-uh	
school year	skōōl yē-uh	
schooner	skōōn-uh	
scimitar	sim-uh-tah	
scissor	siz-uh	
scissors	siz-uhz	
scooter	skōōt-uh	

scorch	skawch	
score	skō-uh	
score board	skō-uh bō-ud	
scoreless	skō-uh-les	
scorn	1) scawn 2) scō-un	
Scorpio	Skaw-pē-ō	Eighth sign of the Zodiac- a water element.
scorpion	skawp-ē-un	
Scottish Terrier	Skot-ish Tār-ē-uh	A black, short, sturdy, bright-eyed terrier.
scour	skow-uh	
scowler	skowl-uh	
screen writer	skrēn rīt-uh	
screw driver	skr ōō drīv-uh	
scripture	skrip-chuh	
script writer	skript rīt-uh	
sculduggery	skul-dug-uh-rē	Shady, maybe even illegal doings.
sculptor	skulp-tuh	
scupper	skup-uh	Opening in the side of the ship so water can drain off the deck.
sea bass	sē bahs	Not bass.
sea farer	sē fār-uh	
sea floor	sē flō-uh	
sea horse	sē hos	
seal	sē-ul	
seaport	sē-pō-ut	
sear	sē-uh	

seashore	sē-shō-uh	
seaward	sē-wud	
seawards	sē-wudz	
second class	sek-und klahs	
sector	sek-tuh	
secular	sek-yōō-luh	Not connected with a church.
secure	suh-kyōō-uh	
seer	sē-uh	One able to tell the future.
seersucker	sē-uh-suk-uh	A crinkled fabric.
seismograph	sīz-mō-grahf	
self centered	self sent-ud	
self important	self im-pō-ut-unt	
self seeker	self sēk-uh	
self support	self suh-pō-ut	
seltzer	selt-zuh	
semaphore	sem-uh-fō-uh	System for signaling.
semester	suh-mes-tuh	
semiconductor	sem-ē-kun-duct-uh	
seminar	sem-in-ah	
semitrailer	sem-ī-trāl-uh	
senator	sen-uh-tuh	
senile	sē-nī-ul	Mind deterioration that goes with old age.
senior	sēn-yuh	
sensor	sen-suh	
September	Sep-tem-buh	9th month of the year.

sequester	suh-kwest-uh	
seraph	sār-uf	One of the highest order of angels.
sergeant	sah-junt	
sergeant major	sah-junt mā-juh	
serial number	sēr-ē-ul num-buh	
server	serv-uh	
service mark	serv-is mahk	
setter	set-uh	
sever	sev-uh	
several	sev-rul	
severe	suh-vē-uh	
sewer	sōō-uh	
sewerage	sōō-uh-rij	
sexual intercourse	sex-yōō-ul in-tuh-kō-us	
shaft	shahft	
shaker	shāk-uh	
Shakespeare, William	Shāks-pē-uh Wil-ē-um	English poet and dramatist. 1564-1616.
shale	shā-ul	Rock of hard clay- flakes easily.
shambles	sham-bulz	Great disorder.
shamrock	sham-rawk	A clover with small leaves in groups of three - the emblem of Ireland.
shan't	shahn't	Shall not.
shard	shahd	A broken piece, often sharp.
share	shā-uh	
share cropper	shā-uh krawp-uh	

share holder	shā-uh hōl-duh	
shark	shahk	
sharp	shahp	
sharpen	shah-pun	
sharp shooter	shahp shōōt-uh	
shatter	shat-uh	
shaver	shāv-uh	A small boy is sometimes called a little shaver.
shear	shē-uh	
sheared or shorn	shē-ud or shawn	
shears	shē-uz	
shebang	shuh-bang	Contrivance- or mainly in the whole shebang.
sheer	shē-uh	Very thin, transparent.
sheik or sheik	shēk or shāk	Chief of an Arab family, tribe, or village.
shell fire	shel fī-uh	
shelter	shel-tuh	
shepherd	shep-ud	
shield	shē-uld	
shimmer	shim-uh	
shiner (slang)	shīn-uh	A black eye.
shin guard	shin gahd	
ship board	ship bō-ud	
ship builder	ship bild-uh	
ship yard	ship yahd	

shire	shī-uh	1) In England, a county. 2) A very large breed of draft horses – the largest.
shiver	shiv-uh	
shock absorber	shawk ub-sob-uh	
shoe horn	sh͞oo hawn	
shoe maker	sh͞oo māk-uh	
shooting star	sh͞oot-in' stah	
shop keeper	shawp kēp-uh	
shop lifter	shawp lift-uh	One who steals from a shop when no one is lookin.
shopper	shawp-uh	
shore	shō-uh	
shorn	1) shō-un 2) shawn	
short	1) shot 2) shawt	
shortage	shawt-ij	
short cut	shawt cut	
shorten	shawt-un	
shortly	shawt-lē	
short order	shawt awd-uh	
short stop	shawt stawp	
short story	shawt staw-rē	
short tempered	shawt temp-ud	
short wave	shawt wāv	

shot	1) shawt 2) shot	Shot and short are pronounced the same in Maine, as the "r" is not pronounced in the word "short". The only way to tell which word is being said is by its context.
shoulder	shōl-duh	
shoulder blade	shōl-duh blād	
shower	show-uh	
show time	shō tīm	WDE: shō tawīm
showy	shō-ē	
shrubbery	shrub-rē	
shudder	shud-uh	
shuffle-board	shuf-ul-bō-ud	
shutter	shut-uh	
shyster	shī-stuh	A deceptive person.
side arm	sīd ahm	
side bar	sīd bah	
side board	sīd bō-ud	
side car	sīd kah	
side splitting	sīd split-in'	A very hearty laughter.
side swiper	sīd swīp-uh	A glancing blow along the side of something.
sight seer	sīt sē-uh	
signature	sig-nuh-chōō-uh	
sign board	sīn bō-ud	
silencer	sī-luns-uh	
silver	sil-vuh	
silverware	sil-vuh-wā-uh	

similar	1) sim-il-uh 2) sim-ul-uh	
simmer	sim-uh	
simper	simp-uh	A silly smile.
sincere	sin-sē-uh	
sinecure	sin-uh-kyo͞o-uh	Income with little or no work.
Singapore	Sing-uh-pō-uh	Island city-state off southern Malaysia.
singular	sing-yo͞o-luh	
sinister	sin-ist-uh	Evil, bad.
sinker	sink-uh	
sinner	sin-uh	One who sins.
sire	sī-uh	
sister	sis-tuh	
sister-in-law	sis-tuh-in-law	Sibling married to one of your brothers.
sitar	sit-ah	A plucked, stringed musical instrument.
six shooter	six sho͞o-tuh	Revolver that holds six bullets.
size skater	sīz skā-tuh	WDE: sawīz skā-tuh
skateboard	skāt-bō-ud	
skedaddle	skē-dad-ul	
skewer	skyo͞o-uh	
skipper	skip-uh	
skitter	skit-uh	
sky lark	skī lahk	
sky scraper	skī skrāp-uh	
skyward	skī-wud	

sky writer	skī rīt-uh	
slacker	slak-uh	No ambition.
slalom	slaw-lum	A ski race marked by poles or flags down a winding course.
slammer	slam-uh	
slander	sland-uh	To lie about someone.
slat	slat	A motion used to force an object off oneself-the motion can also tell someone they should go away.
slather	sla-"th"-uh	Spread on thickly.
slattern	slat-un	Slobbish and immoral woman.
slaughter	slawt-uh	
slave driver	slāv drīv-uh	A cruel overseer.
slaver	slav-uh	To drool.
slavery	slāv-rē	
sleazoid	slēz-ō-ēd	A crass, untrustful person.
sledgehammer	slej-ham-uh	
sleeper	slēp-uh	
sleepover	slēp-ōvuh	
sleep wear	slēp wā-uh	
slender	slend-uh	
slicker	slik-uh	Type of raincoat.
slide fastener	slīd fahs-en-uh	
slider	slīd-uh	
sliding scale	slīd-in' skā-ul	
slip cover	slip cuv-uh	

slipper	slip-uh	
slither	sli-"th"-uh	
sliver	sliv-uh	
slobber	slawb-uh	
slugger	slug-uh	
sluggard	slug-ud	Lazy, sluggish person.
slumber	slum-buh	
slum lord (slang)	slum lawd	Owns houses or apartments in poor shape and rents them out.
small arms	smawl ahmz	
smarmy	smah-mē	Insincere flattery.
smart	smaht	
smarten	smaht-un	Sometimes used along with "up"- to "smarten up".
smear	smē-uh	
smelter	smelt-uh	
smidgen	smij-en	Very small amount — less than a bit or even a dite.
smile	smī-ul	
smoke detector	smōk dē-tek-tuh	
smolder	smōl-duh	
smorgasbord	smaw-gas-bō-ud	
smother	smu-"th"-uh	
smoulder	smōl-duh	Barely burnin'.
snack bar	snak bah	
snail	snā-ul	

snapper	snap-uh	
snare	snā-uh	
snarl	snahl	
sneaker	snēk-uh	
sneer	snē-uh	
snicker	snik-uh	
snifter	snif-tuh	
snigger	snig-uh	To snicker.
sniveler	sniv-ul-uh	One who snivels.
snooker (slang)	snook-uh	If you've ever been snookered, you've been fooled, taken for granted, or deceived.
snore	snō-uh	
snorkel	snaw-kul	
snort	snawt	
snow-board	snō-bō-ud	
snow storm	snō stawm	
snow tire	snō tī-uh	
soar	sō-uh	
sober	sō-buh	
soccer	sawk-uh	
soda cracker	sō-duh krak-uh	
soda water	sō-duh waw-tuh	
sodium bicarbonate	sōd-ē-um bī-kah-bun-it	
soft hearted	soft haht-ed	Tenderhearted.
soft ware	soft wā-uh	

solar	sō-lah	
solder	sawd-uh	
soldier	sōl-juh	
soldier of fortune	sōl-juh ov faw-chōōn	
solemn	sol-um	
solicitor	sah-lis-uh-tuh	
somber	sawm-buh	
somersault	sum-uh-salt	
Somerset	Sum-uh-set	County in Maine.
somewhere	sum-wā-uh	
sonar	sō-nah	
songster	song-stuh	
soothsayer	sōōth-sā-uh	
sophomore	sof-mō-uh	
sorcery	saw-suh-rē	
sore	sō-uh	
sort	sawt	
sound barrier	sound bār-ē-uh	
sounding board	soundin' bō-ud	
sour	sow-uh	
source	sō-us	
sour cream	sow-uh krēm	
sourdough	sow-uh-dō	
South Carolina	South Kār-ō-līn-uh	Southeastern state of the USA. (SC) Capital: Columbia.

South Dakota	South Duh-kō-tuh	Midwestern state of the USA. (SD) Capital: Pierre (Pē-ā-uh).
southerly	su-"th"-uh-lē	
southern	su-"th"-un	
southerner	su-"th"-un-uh	Has a charmin' accent.
southward	south-wud	
souvenir	sōō-vun-ē-uh	
space craft	spās krahft	
space heater	spās hēt-uh	
space port	spās pō-ut	
spar	spah	
spare	spā-uh	
spark	spahk	
sparkle	spah-kul	
sparse	spahs	
Sparta	Spah-tuh	Ancient city in S. Greece.
Spartan	Spah-tun	From Sparta- stoic, strong, aggressive warriors in history.
spatter	spat-uh	
speaker	spēk-uh	
spear	spē-uh	
spectacular	spek-tak-yōō-luh	
spectator	spek-tā-tuh	
specter	spek-tuh	Ghostly being.
speedometer	spē-dawm-uh-tuh	
speedster	spēd-stuh	

spell checker	spel chek-uh	
spelunker	spē-lunk-uh	
sphere	sfē-uh	
spheroid	sfē-uh-rōyd	
sphincter	sfink-tuh	
spider	spī-duh	
spinal cord	spī-nul kawd	
spin doctor (slang)	spin dok-tuh	A political spokesperson.
spinster	spin-stuh	An older unmarried woman.
spiny lobster	spī-nē lob-stuh	
spire	spī-uh	
spit fire	spit fī-uh	
splatter	splat-uh	
splendor	splen-duh	
splinter	splin-tuh	
splutter	splut-uh	1) Spitting/sputter sounds. 2) To speak quickly and confusedly
spoil	spō-ē-ul	
spoil sport	spō-ē-ul spō-ut	
spoliation	spōl-ē-ā-shun	This is said in Maine as it is everywhere. It just isn't used often. It means to rob or be plundering.
sponge bath	spunj bahth	
sponsor	spawn-suh	
spore	spō-uh	
sport	spō-ut	

sports car	spō-uts kah	
sports cast	spō-uts kast	
sportsman	spō-uts-mun	
sporty	spō-ut- ē	
sprayer	sprā-uh	
spring board	spring bō-ud	
spring fever	spring fē-vuh	
sprinter	sprin-tuh	
spume	spyōōm	This is a new word to me even though it describes the foam and froth that happens when the ocean is tossing wildly over rocks or near the shore.
sputter	sput-uh	
squad car	skwod kah	
squalor	skwol-uh	
squander	skwond-uh	
square	skwā-uh	
square dance	skwā-uh dans	Lots of fun!
squeaker	skwēk-uh	
squeal	skwē-ul	
squire	skwī-uh	
staffer	staf-uh	
stair	stā-uh	
staircase	stā-uh-kās	
stair way	stā-uh wā	
stale	stā-ul	

stale mate	stā-ul māt	
stalwart	stawl-wut	
stammer	stam-uh	
standard	stand-ud	
standard bearer	stan-dud bā-uh-ruh	
standardize	stan-dud-īz	
standard time	stan-dud tīm	WDE: stan-dud tawīm
star	stah	
star-board	stah-bud	The right hand side of a ship as you face forward toward the bow.
starch	stahch	
star crossed	stah krawst	This situation does not bode well for those involved.
stardom	stah-dum	
stare	stā-uh	
star fish	stah fish	Sea life shaped like a star.
star gazer	stah gā-zuh	
stark	stahk	
starless	stah-les	
starlet	stah-let	
star light	stah līt	
starling	1) stah-ling 2) stah-lin'	A type of bird.
Star of David	Stah ov Dā-vid	Judaic symbol- six-pointed star.
starry	stah-rē	
Stars and Stripes	Stahz and Strīps	Another name for Old Glory- the American Flag.

star struck	stah struk
start	staht
startle	staht-ul
start-up	staht-up
starve	stahv
Star Wars	Stah Wauz
state of the art	stāt ov "th"ē aht
stature	stach-uh
staying power	stā-in' pow-uh
St. Christopher	Sānt Kris-tuh-fuh
steadfast	sted-fahst
steal	stē-ul
steamer	stēm-uh
steam fitter	stēm fit-uh
steam roller	stēm rōl-uh
steel yard	stēl yahd
steer	stē-uh
stellar	stel-uh
stem ware	stem wā-uh
step brother	step bru-"th"-uh
step ladder	step lad-uh
step sister	step sis-tuh
-ster	stuh	A suffix for one who creates or is associated with- like a roadstuh or huckstuh, etc.
stevedore	stēv-uh-dō-uh

steward	stōō-wud
stewardess	stōō-ud-es
sticker	stik-uh
stickler	stik-luh
still born	1) stil bawn 2) stil bō-un
stinger	sting-uh
stock broker	stok brō-kuh
stock car	stok kah
stock holder	stok hōl-duh
stock yard	stok yahd
stone ware	stōn wā-uh
stop over	stop ō-vuh
stopper	stop-uh
store	stō-uh
store keeper	stō-uh kēp-uh
stork	stawk
storm	stawm
storm door	stawm dō-uh
stormy	stawm-ē
story board	staw-rē bō-ud
story teller	staw-rē tel-uh
stout hearted	stowt haht-ed
straggler	strag-luh
straight forward	strāt faw-wud

straight shooter	strāt shōōt-uh	
strainer	strān-uh	
stranger	strānj-uh	
stratosphere	strat-us-fē-uh	
streamer	strēm-uh	
street car	strēt kah	
street smart	strēt smaht	
street walker	strēt wawk-uh	
stretcher	strech-uh	
stricture	strik-chuh	
stringer	string-uh	
stripper	strip-uh	
stroller	strōl-uh	
strong-arm	strong-ahm	
structure	struk-chuh	
stubborn	stub-un	
studio apartment	stōō-dē-ō uh-paht-munt	
stupor	stōōp-uh	
stutter	stut-uh	
style	stī-ul	To cause someone to commit perjury.
subculture	sub-kul-chuh	
sub marginal	sub mah-jin-ul	
subnormal	sub-naw-mul	
suborbital	sub-awb-it-ul	To help — give aid.
subordinate	sub-awd-in-it	

suborn	sub-un	
substandard	sub-stan-dud	
substructure	sub-struk-chuh	
successor	suk-ses-uh	
succor	suk-uh	
sucker	suk-uh	
suffer	suf-uh	
sugar	1) shuh-guh 2) shu-guh	
suitor	soo-tuh	
sulfur	sul-fuh	
sulphur	sul-fuh	
summer	sum-uh	Warmest of the four seasons.
sunbather	sun-bā-"th"-uh	
sunder	sun-duh	
sunflower	sun-flow-uh	
super	soo-puh	A common word expressing excitement.
super cargo	soo-puh kah-gō	
super charge	soo-puh chahj	
super conductor	soo-puh kun-duct-uh	
superfluous	soo-per-floo-us	
superior	soo-pēr-ē-uh	
superlative	soo-purl-uh-tiv	
superman	soo-puh-man	
supermarket	soo-puh-mahk-it	

supernal	sōō-per-nul	
supernumerary	sōō-puh-noom-uh-rā-rē	
super power	sōō-puh pow-uh	
super star	sōō-puh stah	
superstore	sōō-puh-stō-uh	
super structure	sōō-puh strukt-chuh	
super tanker	sōō-puh tank-uh	
supper	sup-uh	
support	suh-pō-ut	
Supreme Court	Sōō-prēm Cō-ut	
surcharge	sur-chahj	
sure	1) shō-uh 2) shōō-uh	
sure fire	1) shō-uh fī-uh 2) shōō-uh fī-uh	
surf board	surf bō-ud	
surgery	1) sur-juh-rē 2) surj-rē	
surpass	sur-pahs	
surrender	sur-end-uh	
surveying	sur-vā-in'	A good example of how a Mainer drops the "g" of "ing".
survivor	sur-vī-vuh	
suspenders	su-spend-uz	
sutler	sut-luh	Not commonly used anymore, as it used to be "a person following an army to sell the soldiers things".
suture	sōō-chuh	

swagger	swag-uh	
swarm	swawm	Things swarm, like bees after their queen.
swarthy	swah-"th"-ē	
swashbuckler	swawsh-buk-luh	
swear, swore	swā-uh, swō-uh	swā-uh-rin'
swearer	swā-uh-ruh	
sweat	swet	
sweater	swet-uh	Clothing for the upper body, usually made of yarn.
sweetbrier	swēt-brī-uh	
sweet corn	swēt kawn	
sweetener	swēt-en-uh	
sweet heart	swēt haht	
sweet pepper	swēt pep-uh	
swinger	swing-uh	
Swiss chard	Swis chahd	
switch board	swich bō-ud	
switch hitter	swich hit-uh	
sword	sō-ud	
sword fish	sō-ud fish	
swore	swō-uh	
sycamore	sik-uh-mō-uh	Trees.
synergism	sin-uh-jiz-um	
synthesizer	sin-thuh-sīz-uh	

Twentieth letter of the English Alphabet T,t (tē)

Word	Pronunciation Examples	Notes
tabernacle	tab-uh-nak-ul	
table tennis	tā-bul ten-is	
table ware	tā-bul wā-uh	
tabular	tab-yōō-luh	
tachometer	tak-awm-i-tuh	
tachycardia	tak-uh-kahd-ē-uh	
taco	tah-kō	
taff rail	taf rā-ul	A rail around the ship's stern.
Taft, William Howard	Taft, Wil-yum How-ud	27th President of the USA.
tail	tā-ul	
tailor	tā-luh	
take over	tāk ōv-uh	
tale	tāl	
tale bearer	tāl bār-uh	
Tallahassee	Tal-uh-has-ē	Capital of Florida.
tam-o' shanter	tam-ō' shan-tuh	A Scottish cap.
tamper	tamp-uh	
tanager	tan-uh-juh	Small songbirds.
tan bark	tan bahk	
tankard	tank-ud	Large cup with a handle.
tanker	tank-uh	
tanner	tan-uh	

taper	tā-puh	
tape recorder	tāp rē-kawd-uh	
tar	tah	
tardy	tah-dē	Being late.
target	tah-get	
tarmac	tah-mak	
tarnish	tah-nish	
tarot	tā-rō	Cards used to foresee the future, and other things, too.
tarp	tahp	
tarpaulin	tah-pawl-in	A sheet of waterproofed canvass.
tarpon	tah-pun	Game fish of W. Atlantic.
tart	taht	
tartan	tah-tun	
tartar	tah-tuh	A deposit that forms on teeth.
tartar sauce	tah-tuh saws	You can make some with mayo and pickle relish.
task force	task fō-us	
task master	1) task mast-uh 2) task mahst-uh	
tatter	tat-uh	
tattered	tat-ud	
tattle	tat-ul	
tattle tale	tat-ul tā-ul	
tavern	tav-un	
taxi meter	tax-ē mē-tuh	

tax payer	tax pā-uh	
tax shelter	tax shel-tuh	
Taylor, Zachary	Tā-luh, Zak-uh-rē	12th President of the USA.
teacher	tē-chuh	
teamster	tēm-stuh	
tear (tore, torn, tearing)	tā-uh (tō-uh, tō-un, tār-in')	
tear	tē-uh	Salty fluid that drips from one's eyes (crying).
tears	tē-uz	
tear drop	tē-uh drawp	
tear gas	tē-uh gas	
tear jerker	tē-uh jerk-uh	A situation causing one to cry.
teaser	tēz-uh	
Technicolor	Tek-ni-kul-uh	
teddy bear	ted-ē bā-uh	
teeter	tē-tuh	Unstable, wobble.
teeter-totter	tē-tuh-tawt-uh	
teetotaler	tē-tot-ul-uh	Never drinks an alcoholic beverage.
telegraph	tel-eh-grahf	
telemarketing	tel-uh-mah-kit-in'	
teleprompter	tel-uh-prawmp-tuh	
teletypewriter	tel-uh-tīp-rīt-uh	
teller	tel-uh	
temblor	tem-bluh	To tremble.

temper	temp-uh	
temperament	temp-uh-ment	Someone's disposition.
temperance	tem-puh-runs	1) Abstinence from alcohol. 2) Moderation, in general.
temperature	tem-puh-ch$\overline{oo}$-uh	
tempered	temp-ud	
tenant farmer	ten-ant fahm-uh	
tender	tend-uh	
tender foot	tend-uh foot	
tender hearted	tend-uh haht-ed	
tenderloin	tend-uh-lō-ēn	
Tennessee	Ten-uh-sē	A state of the US. (TN) Capital: Nashville.
tenor	ten-uh	Highest range of the male voice.
tenter hook	ten-tuh hook	Hooked nail.
tenure	ten-yuh	
terrain	tuh-rān	
terranium	ter-ān-ē-um	
terrazzo	tuh-rah-zō	Flowing of marble chips.
terrible	tār-uh-bul	
terrier	tār-ē-uh	
terrific	tuh-rif-ik	
terrify	tār-i-fī	WDE: tār-uh-fawī
territory	tār-uh-taw-rē	
terror	tār-uh	
terrorism	tār-uh-izm	

testator	tes-tā-tuh	One who has made their will.
tether	te-"th"-uh	
tetra	tet-ruh	
tetrameter	tet-ram-i-tuh	A certain rhythm for some poetic verse.
Texas	Tex-us	Southwest state of the USA. (TX) Capital: Augusta. Great accent there, too!
texture	tex-chuh	
theater	1) thē-i-tuh 2) thē-āt-tuh 3) thē-et-uh	
their	"th"-ā-uh	
theirs	"th"-ā-uhz	
theory	1) thē-rē 2) thē-uh-rē	
therapy	thār-uh-pē	
there	"th"-ā-uh	
thereafter	"th"-ā-uh-ahft-uh	
therefore	"th"-ā-uh-fō-uh	
thermometer	1) thuh-mom-uh-tuh 2) ther-mom-uh-tuh	
thermonuclear	thermō-nōō-klē-uh	
theta	thā-tuh	8th letter of Greek alphabet.
they	"th"-ā	
thinner	thin-uh	
thither	thi-"th"-uh	Toward a place to "come thither".
Thor	1) Thaw 2) Thō-uh	Mythical god of thunder and war.
thorn	thawn	

thorough fare	thurō fā-uh	Public main street.
thrasher	thrash-uh	
threadbare	thred-bā-uh	
three decker	thrē dek-uh	
three R's	thrē Ah'z	Reading, Writing, and Arithmetic.
three score	thrē skō-uh	A score: 20. Three score: 60.
thunder	thun-duh	
thunder bolt	thun-duh bolt	
thunder head	thun-duh hed	
thunder shower	thun-duh show-uh	
thunder storm	thun-duh stawm	
thunder struck	thun-duh struk	It happens when one is shocked suddenly with great surprise or even fear.
thwart	thwawt	A seat across a boat – or when a person's plans are defeated.
ticker	tik-uh	
tickler	1) tik-luh 2) tik-ul-uh	
tide water	tīd wot-uh	WDE- tawīd wotuh
tie breaker	tī brāk-uh	
tier	tē-uh	It's not unusual to see a number of tē-uhz on a cake.
tiger	tī-guh	
tipster	tip-stuh	
tire	tī-uh	
tired	tī-ud	
tire iron	tī-uh ī-un	

tireless	tī-uh-les	
tiresome	tī-uh-sum	
tissue paper	ti-shōō pāp-uh	
title holder	tī-tul hōld-uh	
titter	tit-uh	A stifled laugh or giggle.
toaster	tōs-tuh	
toastmaster	1) tōst-mas-tuh 2) tōst-mahs-tuh	
toddler	tawd-luh	
together	tōō-ge-"th"-uh	
toilet paper	tō-ē-let pā-puh	
Tokyo	Tō-kē-ō	
tomato	tuh-mā-tō	
tone arm	tōn ahm	The pivoting arm in the old fashioned record player.
toner	tō-nuh	
tongue	tung	There's a lot to say about a tongue. It is the muscular structure in your mouth that makes it possible to form words, manage food and fluid, helps to whistle, and carries the little "bumps" that house your taste buds. It also allows you to lick something, helps in kissing - and it can stick out to be fresh.
tongue twister	tung twist-uh	
tooth powder	tōōth pow-duh	
top brass	tawp brahs	
top drawer	tawp draw	In Maine, the "er" is silent in this word.
Topeka	Tō-pēk-uh	Capital of Kansas.
toper	top-uh	

227

topsail	tawp sā-ul	
Torah or Tora	Tor-uh	
torch	tawch	
torch bearer	tawch bār-uh	
toreador	taw-rē-uh-dō-uh	
torment	taw-ment	
tornado	taw-nā-dō	
torpedo	taw-pē-dō	
torpid	taw-pid	Sluggish, dull.
torpor	taw-puh	Dullness.
torque	tō-uk	A force that acts to produce rotation.
torrent	taw-runt	
torrid	taw-rid	Passionate.
torsion	taw-shun	A twisting force.
torso	taw-sō	
tort	tawt	
torte	tō-ut	A very tasty pastry.
tortellini	taw-tul-ēnē	
tortilla	taw-tē-uh	
tortoise	tawt-us	A large turtle.
tortuous	taw-chōō-us	
torture	taw-chuh	
totter	tawt-uh	
tour	tō-uh	
tour de force	tōōr duh fō-us	

tourism	1) to͞or-izm	
	2) tor-izm	
tourist	tor-ist	People visiting an area for a vacation.
tourmaline	to͞or-muh-lēn	
tournament	tor-nuh-ment	
tourniquet	turn-i-ket	
toward	to-wud	
tower	tow-uh	
town crier	town krī-uh	
tracery	trās-uh-rē	
track record	trak rek-ud	
tractor	trak-tuh	
tractor trailer	trak-tuh trā-luh	
trade mark	trād mahk	
trader	trād-uh	
trail blazer	trā-ul blāz-uh	
trailer	trā-ul-uh	
trailer park	trāl-uh pahk	
traitor	trāt-uh	
trajectory	truh-ject-uh-rē	
tranquilizer	trank-wil-īz-uh	
transceiver	trans-ēv-uh	
transducer	trans-do͞os-uh	
transfer	trans-fer	One of the few words where the "r" is pronounced at the end of the word.
transfigure	trans-fig-yuh	

229

transform	trans-fawm	
transformer	trans-fawm-uh	
transition	trans-i-shun	
transliterate	trans-lit-uh-rit	
transmitter	trans-mit-uh	
transpire	trans-pī-uh	
transponder	trans-pawn-duh	
transport	trans-pō-ut	
trap door	trap dō-uh	
trawler	trawl-uh	
treasure	tre-"zh"-uh	
treasury	tre-"zh"-uh-rē	
tremor	trem-uh	
trencher	trench-uh	
Trenton	Trent-un	Capital of New Jersey – also a town on the mainland just before you go on to Mount Desert Island.
trespass	tres-pahs	
trial and error	trī-ul and ār-uh	
trick or treater	trik aw trēt-uh	
trickster	trik-stuh	
tricolor	trī-kul-uh	
trigger	trig-uh	
trimaran	trī-muh-ran	A boat like a catamaran but has three hulls.
trimester	trī-mes-tuh	
trip hammer	trip ham-uh	

Trojan Horse	Trō-jun Hos	
trolley car	trawl-ē kah	
troposphere	trop-uhs-fē-uh	The part of the atmosphere that controls our weather.
troubadour	trōō-buh-dō-uh	
trouble maker	trub-ul māk-uh	
trouble shooter	trub-ul shōō-tuh	
trouper	trōō-puh	
trucker	truk-uh	
truck farm	truk fahm	
true believer	trōō buh-lēv-uh	
Truman, Harry S.	Trōō-mun, Har-ē Es.	33rd President of the USA.
tsar	zah	Alternate spelling is Czar.
T square	Tē skwā-uh	
tuber	tōō-buh	
tubercle	tōō-buh-kul	
tubular	tōōb-yōō-luh	
tucker	tuk-uh	
Tuesday	1) Tōōz-dā 2) Tōōz-dē	For some reason, a Mainer will often turn the "a" in "day" into the "e" sound when pronouncing the days of the week.
tug of war	tug ov waw	
tumbler	tum-bluh	
tumor	tōō-muh	
tuning fork	tōōn-in' fawk	
turban	tur-bun	

turbo charge	tur-bō chahj	
turbulent	ter-byōō-lunt	
turkey vulture	terkē vulch-uh	
turkey buzzard	ter-kē buz-ud	
Turkish bath	Terkish bahth	
turnover	tern-ōvuh	
turner	tern-uh	
turquoise	1) terk-ō-is 2) terk-ō-ēs	
tussock	tus-uk	
tutor	tōō-tuh	
TV dinner	Tē-Vē din-uh	
twaddle	twawd-ul	Nonsense.
'tween	'twēn	
tweezers	twēz-uz	
twiddle	twid-ul	Fiddle with something.
twirler	twerl-uh	
twister	twist-uh	
twitter	twit-uh	
two by four	tōō bī fō-uh	A piece of lumber called 2"x4" but is actually 1.5"x3.5"
two-fer	tōō-fuh	Two things sold for the price of one.
Tyler, John	Tī-luh, Jon	10th President of the USA.
type setter	tīp set-uh	
type writer	tīp rīt-uh	
typhoid fever	tī-fō-ēd fēv-uh	

typographer	1) tī-pō-grahf-uh
	2) tī-pawg-ruh-fuh
tyrannosaur	tī-ran-ō-saw
tzar	zah

Twenty-First letter of the English Alphabet U,u (yōō)

Word	Pronunciation Examples	Notes
udder	u-duh	Where the cow holds milk.
ufology	yōō-fōl-uh-jē	Study of unidentified flying objects (UFOs).
ulcer	ul-suh	
ulcerate	ul-suh-rāt	
ulster	ul-stuh	A long, warm overcoat worn in Northern Ireland.
ulterior	ul-tēr-ē-uh	
ultra	ul-truh	
ultra marine	ul-truh muh-rēn	Deep blue.
ultra violet	ul-truh vī-let	
umbra	um-bruh	Shade or shadow.
umpire	um-pī-uh	
unadorned	un-uh-dawnd	
unadulterated	un-uh-dul-tuh-rāt-ed	
unanswered	un-ans-ud	
unarmed	un-ahmd	
unasked	un-ahskt	
unaware	un-uh-wā-uh	

unawares	un-uh-wā-uz	
unbar	un-bah	
unbearable	un-bā-uh-ruh-bul	
unbelievable	un-be-lēv-uh-bul	
unbeliever	un-bē-lēv-uh	
unborn	1) un-bawn 2) un-bō-un	
uncared for	un-cā-ud faw	
uncensored	un-sen-sud	
uncharted	un-chaht-ed	
unclear	un-klē-uh	
uncomfortable	un-kum-fut-uh-bul	
uncork	un-cawk	
uncover	un-kuv-uh	
under	un-duh	
underachiever	un-duh-uh-chēv-uh	
underact	un-duh-akt	
underage	un-duh-āj	Below the age that is required by law.
underarm	un-duh-ahm	
under belly	un-duh bel-ē	
underbid	un-duh-bid	
undercharge	un-duh-chahj	
underclass	un-duh-klahs	
underclassman	un-duh-klahs-mun	
undercover	un-duh-kuv-uh	

undergarment	un-duh-gah-munt
underpass	un-duh-pahs
underperform	un-duh-puh-fawm
underscore	un-duh-sko-uh
undershorts	un-duh-shawts
understaffed	un-duh-stahft
undertaker	un-duh-tāk-uh
under-the-counter	un-duh-"th"uh-kown-tuh Done illegally.
underwater	un-duh-wot-uh
underwear	un-duh-wā-uh
undiscovered	un-dis-kuv-ud
unexpired	un-eks-pī-ud
unexplored	un-eks-plō-ud
unfair	un-fā-uh
unfamiliar	un-fuh-mil-ē-uh
unforeseen	1) un-faw-sēn 2) un-fō-uh-sēn
unforgivable	un-faw-giv-uh-bul
unforgotten	1) un-fō-uh-got-un 2) un-fuh-gut-un
unguarded	un-gahd-ed
unhampered	un-hamp-ud
unharmed	un-hahmd
unhorsed	1) un-hosed 2) un-host
unicorn	yōō-nuh-kawn

uniform	yōō-nuh-fawm
unimpaired	un-im-pā-ud
unimportant	un-im-paw-tunt
unincorporated	un-in-kaw-puh-rāt-ed
uninformed	un-in-fawmd
uninjured	un-in-jud
uninspired	un-in-spī-ud
uninsure	un-in-shōō-uh
uninsured	un-in-shō-ud
United Nations	Yōō-nīt-ed Nā-shunz
United States	Yōō-nīt-ed Stāts
unlettered	un-let-ud
unlimber	un-lim-buh
unmannerly	un-man-uh-lē
unmarked	un-mahkt
unnumbered	un-num-bud
unpardonable	un-pah-dun-uh-bul
unpopular	un-pop-yōō-luh
unprepared	un-prē-pā-ud
unrecorded	un-rē-kawd-ed
unsnarl	un-snahl
unstructured	un-struk-shud
unsupervised	un-sōōp-uh-vīzd
unsure	1) un-shōō-uh 2) un-shō-uh

unsurpassed	un-suh-pahst	
untarnished	un-tah-nishd	Not sullied nor marred.
untoward	un-tō-ud	
untutored	un-tōō-tud	
upholster	2) up-hōls-tuh 2) uh-pōl-stuh	
upmarket	up-mah-ket	
upper	up-uh	
upper case	up-uh kās	
upper class	up-uh klahs	
uprear	up-rē-uh	
upriver	up-riv-uh	
uproar	up-rō-uh	
up stairs	up stā-uz	
upstart	up-staht	
upward	up-wud	
ureter	1) yur-ē-tuh 2) ur-et-uh	
user	yōōz-uh	
usher	ush-uh	
utmost	ut-mōst	The very, very most.
utter	ut-uh	
uttermost	ut-uh-mōst	

Twenty-Second letter of the English Alphabet V,v (vē)

Word	Pronunciation Examples	Notes
vacuum cleaner	vak-yōōm klēn-uh	
Valley Forge	Val-ē Fawj	A village in SE Pensylvania-scene of George Washington's winter encampment (1777-78)
valor	val-uh	
vampire	vam-pī-uh	
vampire bat	vam-pī-uh bat	
Vandyke	Van-dīk	Type of "bē-ud" (beard).
van-guard	van-gahd	
vapor	vā-puh	
varicolored	vā-rē-kul-ud	
variety store	vuh-rī-uh-tē stō-uh	
varmint or varmit	vah-munt or vah-mit	
varnish	vah-nish	
varsity	vah-sit-ē	
vascular	vask-yōō-lah	
vasomotor	vāz-ō-mōt-uh	
vector	vek-tuh	
veer	vē-uh	
velour	vul-ō-uh	
ventilator	vent-il-ā-tuh	
venture	ven-chuh	
venturesome	ven-chuh-sum	

verger	verj-uh	
vermiform	ver-mi-fawm	Worm-shaped.
Vermont	Ver-mawnt	New England State of the USA. (VT) Capital: Mont-pelier.
vernacular	vur-nak-yōō-lah	
vernier	vern-ē-uh	
vespers	ves-puz	Evening prayers.
veterinary	vet-uh-nār-ē	
vicar	vik-ah	
vinegar	vin-ig-uh	
vineyard	1) vin-yud 2) vin-yahd	
vitner	vit-nuh	
viper	vīp-uh	
visitor	viz-it-uh	
visor	vīz-uh	
vocal cords	1) vō-kul cō-udz 2) vō-kul cawdz	
voice over	vō-ēs ō-vuh	
Voltaire	Vol-tā-uh	French writer.
voltmeter	vōlt-mē-tuh	
volunteer	vol-un-tē-uh	
voucher	vow-chuh	
vulgar	vul-guh	
vulture	vul-chuh	

Twenty-Third letter of the English Alphabet W,w (dubl-y$\overline{oo}$)

Word	Pronunciation Examples	Notes
wader	wād-uh	
wafer	wā-fuh	
wager	wā-juh	
waiter	wā-tuh	
waiver	wāv-uh	
Waldo	Wold-ō	County in Maine.
walker	waw-kuh	
wall board	wol bō-ud	
wall flower	wol flow-uh	
wallpaper	wol-pā-puh	
wander	won-duh	
wanderer	won-duh-ruh	
war	waw	
warbler	waw-bluh	
war crime	waw krīm	
ward	wawd	
warden	waw-dun	
wardrobe	wawd-rōb	
ware	wā-uh	
warehouse	wā-uh-hows	
warfare	waw-fā-uh	
warhorse	waw-hos	

warlock	waw-lawk
warlord	waw-lawd
warm	wawm
warmer	wawm-uh
warmed over	wawmd ō-vuh
warm front	wawm frunt
warmhearted	wawm-haht-ed
warmonger	waw-mong-uh
warmth	wawmth
warm up	wawm up
warn	wawn
warning	wawn-in'
warp	wawp
war path	waw pahth
warp speed	wawp spēd
warrant	waw-runt
warrant officer	waw-runt awf-is-uh
warranty	waw-an-tē
warren	waw-run
warrior	waw-yuh
warship	waw-ship
wart	wawt
wary	wār-ē
wash and wear	1) wawsh and wā-uh 2) wosh and wā-uh

washboard	1) wawsh-bō-ud 2) wosh-bō-ud	
washer	1) wawsh-uh 2) wosh-uh	
Washington	Wosh-ing-tun	1) County in Maine. 2) NW coastal state of the USA. (WA) Capital: Olympia. 3) Washington D.C. Capital of the USA.
Washington, George	No change.	First President of the USA.
wastebasket	wāst-bahs-kit	
wastepaper	wāst-pā-puh	
watchtower	woch-tow-uh	
water	wo-tuh	
watercolor	wot-uh kul-uh	
watercourse	wot-uh-kō-us	
watercraft	wot-uh-krahft	
watermark	wot-uh-mahk	
water power	wot-uh pow-uh	
water tower	wot-uh tow-uh	
watery	wot-uh-rē	
waver	wāv-uh	
wax paper	waks pā-puh	
way farer	wā fār-uh	
wayward	wā-wud	

wear
  (worn,
    wore)
	1) wā-uh
	2) wawn
	3) wō-uh	

wear and tear	wā-uh and tā-uh	

weather	we-"th"-uh	
weather beaten	we-"th"-uh bē-tun	
weathering	we-"th"-uh-rin'	
weatherize	we-"th"-uh-rīz	
Webster, Noah	Web-stuh, Nō-uh	(1758-1843) a United States lexicographer.
weir	wē-uh	
weird	wē-ud	Mysterious, odd.
weirdo (slang)	wē-ud-ō	Someone who is weird.
welfare	wel-fā-uh	
wellborn	1) wel-bawn 2) wel-bō-un	
well informed	wel in-fawmd	
well mannered	wel man-uhd	
well wisher	wel wish-uh	
well worn	wel wō-un	
welter	wel-tuh	
welter weight	wal-tuh wāt	A boxer with a max weight of 147 lbs.
we're	wē-uh	We are.
werewolf	wē-uh wulf	Folklore.
westerly	west-uh-lē	
western	west-un	
westerner	west-un-uh	

Western
  Hemisphere
	West-un
	  Hem-is-fē-uh	

westernize	west-un-īz	

westward	west-wud	
whale	1) wāl 2) wā-ul	
whaler	1) wāl-uh 2) wā-ul-uh	
wharf	wawf	
whatever	wut-ev-uh	
whatsoever	wut-sō-ev-uh	
wheel	wē-ul	
wheelbarrow	wē-ul-bār-ō	
wheelchair	wē-ul-chā-uh	
wheeler dealer	wē-ul-uh dēl-uh	
whenever	wen-ev-uh	
where	1) wā-uh 2) wār	
wherefore	wā-uh-fō-uh	
whomever	hōōm-ev-uh	
whopper	waw-puh	
whore	hō-uh	
who-so-ever	hōō-sō-ev-uh	
wicked	wik-id	Has dual definitions: 1) Something terrible, as from the Devil. 2) Something very, very special, especially good. It depends on the context.
wicker	wik-uh	
wide	wīd	WDE: wawīd
widower	wid-ō-uh	Married man's wife died.
wiener	wēn-uh	A hotdog.

wilderness	1) wil-duh-nes 2) wool-duh-nes	
wild fire	wī-uld fī-uh	
wild flower	wī-uld flow-uh	
wile	wīl	
willpower	wil-pow-uh	
Wilson, Woodrow	No change.	28th President of the USA.
Winchester	Win-chest-uh	Trademark of a particular repeating rifle that "won the west".
wind breaker	wind brāk-uh	
wind-chill factor	wind-chil fak-tuh	
wind farm	wind fahm	
wind jammer	wind jam-uh	Large sailing ship.
window dresser	wid-ō dres-uh	
wind shear	wind shē-uh	
wind storm	wind stawm	
windward	wind-wud	
wine colored	wīn kul-ud	Dark purplish.
winery	wīn-uh-rē	
winner	win-uh	
winter	win-tuh	
winter beater	win-tuh bēt-uh	A car that's older and not in great shape BUT good enough to get you through the winter.
winterize	win-tuh-rīz	
wire	wī-uh	
wired	wī-ud	

wire hair	wī-uh hā-uh	
Wisconsin	Wis-kon-sun	Midwest state of the USA. (WI) Capital: Madison.
wise acre	wīz āk-uh	
wisecrack	wīz-krak	
witch craft	wich crahft	
witch doctor	wich doc-tuh	
witchery	wich-uh-rē	
wither	wi-"th"-uh	
withers	wi-"th"-uz	Between a horse's shoulders.
wizard	wiz-ud	
wizardry	wiz-ud-rē	
wolverine	wul-vuh-rēn	
wonder	wund-uh	
wonderful	1) wund-uh-ful 2) wun-duh-ful	
wondrous	wun-drus	
wood carver	wud kahv-uh	
woodcraft	wud-krahft	
woodcutter	wud-kut-uh	
woodpecker	wud-pek-uh	
wood pile	wud pī-ul	Often seen in Maine.
woofer	wuf-uh	A large speaker.
word	werd	
word of honor	werd ov ohn-uh	
word processor	werd praw-ses-uh	

wrecker	rek-uh
wringer	ring-uh
writer	rīt-uh
Wyoming	Wī-ōm-in'

Wyoming: Mountain state of the Western USA. (WY) (Wind River Mts) Capital: Cheyenne.

wore	wō-uh
worker	werk-uh
workfare	werk-fā-uh
workforce	werk-fō-us
workhorse	werk-hos
World War	Werld Waw
worm gear	werm gē-uh
worn	wō-un
worn out	wō-un owt
worrywart	wur-ē-wot
wrangler	1) rang-ul-uh 2) rang-luh
wrapper	rap-uh

worrywart: One who worries excessively.

Twenty-Fourth letter of the English Alphabet X,x (eks)

Word	Pronunciation Examples	Notes
Xenon	Zē-non	
Xerography	Zer-awg-ruh-fē	
Xerox	Zēr-ox	

Twenty-Fifth letter of the English Alphabet Y,y (wī)

Word	Pronunciation Examples	Notes
yacht	yawt	
yachting	yawt-in'	
Yahweh	Yah-wā	Hebrew name for Almighty God.
yammer	yam-uh	Continuous jabber.
Yank (slang)	Yank	A Yankee, especially a US soldier in WWI, WWII, and the Civil War.
Yankee	Yank-ē	A New Englander.
yard	yahd	
yardage	yahd-ij	
yardarm	yahd-ahm	Support for a sail.
yarn	yahn	
yatter	yat-uh	
Y chromosome	Wī krō-mō-sōm	Identifies the person as being male.
yeah	1) yā-uh 2) yuh	Means yes or okay – similar to ayuh.
year	yē-uh	
yearling	yē-uh-lin'	An animal in its second year.
year round	yē-uh rownd	
yea sayer	yā sā-uh	Optimistic towards life.
yellow fever	yel-ō fē-vuh	
yesterday	1) yes-tuh-dā 2) yest-uh-dē	
yesteryear	yes-tuh-yē-uh	Distant past.

yield	yē-uld	
yogurt	yō-gut	
yonder	yawn-duh	
Yonkers	Yawnk-uz	City in SW New York.
yore	yō-uh	Long ago.
York	Yawk	Southern county in Maine.
youngster	yung-stuh	A kid.
your	yō-uh	
yours	1) yō-uz 2) yawz	
your self	yō-uh self	
yourselves	1) yaw-selvz 2) yō-uh-selvz	
yuck	yuk	Something unpleasant.
yuk (slang)	yuk	A good laugh.

Twenty-Sixth letter of the English Alphabet Z,z (zē or zed)

Word	Pronunciation Examples	Notes
Zanzibar	Zan-zuh-bah	An island off the East coast.
zeal	zē-ul	
zephyr	zef-uh	
zero hour	zē-rō ow-uh	
Zig Zag	No change.	A famous brand of rolling papers to form your own smokes.
zinger (slang)	zing-uh	Witty - a good joke.
zipper	zip-uh	

zither	zi-"th"-uh	Various stringed musical instruments like a dulcimer.
Zuni	Zōō-nē	Pueblo-dwellin' Native American people of West New Mexico.
zymurgy	Zim-uh-jē	Chemistry of fermentation applied in brewing, etc.

Counties of Maine

Androscoggin	An-drō-skog-in
Aroostook	Uh-rōōs-tick
Cumberlin	Kum-buh-lin
Franklin	Frank-lin
Hancock	Han-kawk
Kennebec	Ken-ē-bek
Knox	Nox
Lincoln	Link-un
Oxford	Awks-fud
Penobscot	1) Pen-ob-skot 2) Puh-nob-skot
Piscataquis	Pis-cat-uh-qwis
Sagadohoc	Sag-uh-duh-hawk
Somerset	Sum-uh-set
Waldo	Wawl-dō
Washington	Wosh-ing-tun
York	Yawk

Days of the Week Overview

Monday	Mun-dē
Tuesday	Tōōz-dē
Wednesday	Wenz-dē
Thursday	Thurz-dē
Friday	Frī-dē
Saturday	Satuh-dē
Sunday	Sun-dē

Months of the Year Overview

January	Jan-yōō-ār-ē	July	Jōō-lī
February	Feb-yōō-ār-ē	August	Aug-ust
March	Mahch	September	Sep-tem-buh
April	Āprul	October	Ok-tō-buh
May	Mā	November	Nō-vem-buh
June	Jōōn	December	Dē-sem-buh

Wicked Official Down Eastah Test

Did you ever wonder how close you would come to being – or qualifyin' for being – a Down Eastah? Well, here's a bit of fun to find out. The first section has 52 questions. The second section has ten questions but is not scored.

When you start the first part of the test, you will need a piece of paper and something to write with. There are three possible answers:

1) ay-uh (yes, you agree).

2) probly (short for probably) and conveys you most likely would do that or agree with the question.

3) uh–uh is the negative – same as no sir!, disagrees, or wouldn't do it.

For each answer you earn something of the point system. Ayuh earns one point. Probly earns 1/2 point. Uh uh (no!) earns NO points. So, read the 52 questions or statements, put down your answer, then at the end, add up your points and see where you stand.

If you want to read on and see how you feel about those last ten questions, Go ahead! Enjoy!!

W.O. Down Eastah Test

1) Do you find yourself day dreamin' over last summer's love, but feelin' glad – hell, relieved – that it's just a memory? (Those of you who are now married will need to think back to your single days for this one!)

2) You prefer drivin' a time-tested classic vehicle with personality more than a new "off the rack" one.

3) You find yourself saving those little cotton plugs out of the aspirin bottle 'cause they might come in handy for something. After all, it is wicked clean, isn't it?

4) You find an inexplicable tolerance, even attraction, to alcoholics (sober or otherwise).

5) You still use "a bit", "a dite", and a "smidgen" as universal standards of measure.

6) When you see those exercise fanatics on TV, it makes you glad you don't give a shit.

7) You sometimes prefer the smell of salt air (at low tide), the sound of sea gulls, and a good dog over anything else.

8) This winter you're likely to listen to the evening news while sittin' by your wood stove and wishin' you had a pipe stem to chew on.

9) Especially in the summer, as you drive down the road, you envision what it would be like to own a missile launcher, aim it under that unbelievably pokey car in front of you, and – BLAM!!!

10) It makes you more angry every year that the road kill count keeps risin'.

11) Does the increase in road kill make you angry and just want to polish up the .306?

12) You refer to your cats, dogs, and critters in general as members of your household.

13) As you sat in school daydreamin', you wondered just how many classmates might be illegitimate relatives (in secret).

14) You quietly smile to yourself when you (single) hear of a new divorcée – after all, fresh meat for the market! (You may need to think back to your single days?)

15) You have finally become accustomed to all the "new" (in the last 20 years) transmission towers. (Even though you still might like to use them for target practice at times.)

16) You see the peace and beauty of winter as a lifesaving oasis in the middle of the tourism desert <u>rather than</u> freezing, near-dead isolation.

17) You celebrate more to see the tourists leave than when they return.

18) You thank your Higher Power that you get to live in Maine year-round, and <u>still</u> make enough to pay taxes and keep a nip in the liquor cabinet!

19) You all but raised the flag and did the jig when "they" finally let hard liquor be sold in the grocery store AND on Sundays!!

20) You take it quite personal when someone shoots up your yard art!

21) You look forward to the Blue Hill Fair (or <u>your</u> local fair) – after all, you see some pretty strange folks AND some relatives you don't see very often.

22) When someone says "the Net" you assume they're talkin' about the thing you catch eels with. OR, GET OVER IT!

23) Could be that chocolate rates right up there with good lobstuh and great sex.

24) Recently decided that U.F.O. stands for Unbearable Friggin' Outa-Staters.

25) You see the Red Sox, The Bruins, and the Patriots as your hometown teams.

26) You assume "shootin' up" means partial or total destruction by some sort of fire arm – NOT stickin' some foreign substance in a precious appendage.

27) STATEMENT – agree or disagree (ay-uh or uh-uh). It's not that you <u>want</u> to have missin' teeth. It's just a matter of priorities. I mean, weigh it out:
   a) missin' teeth / a new shotgun
   b) missin' teeth / a trip to see the Red Sox
   c) missin' teeth / this summer's supply of Purple Jesus.
   d) missin' teeth / this year's huntin' trip

   NO CONTEST!!! thuh heck with it – just gum it!!!

28) Your main line of work is seasonal and your backup line of work is more fun.

29) Often forget the name of your mate 'cause you've been callin' 'em "dear" (dee -uh) or "darling" (dah-lin), or some other pet name, for SO long.

30) The smell of crisp fall air trigguz that urge to beat the hell out of a tree and burn it. (called splittin' wood for the stove.)

31) I fondly remember the endearing words of my father echoin' out of the past – "Holy cat turd!" (An appropriate expression in any remarkable situation). Then there's "Well, kiss my ass and go to hell"! (An expression any self-respectin' Irishman would save for any outstanding occurrences.) Finally, there's "Oooo Baby", the highest compliment someone of the fairer sex could have! Do you have similar fond memories?

32) Well, with these words of wisdom in mind, you make <u>sure</u> (sho-uh) that you get to the dump at least once a week, 'cause yuh never know what treasures ya might find – OR miss if you don't go.

33) You would rather eat <u>all</u> the tomally (pronounced "Tom-Alley") yourself than share it with the cat. (Tomally is that nice green stuff in the lobster. It's lobster liver!)

Here are some common abbreviations, see if you agree with the definitions.

34) A.A.A. = Available Anytime, Anywhere

35) Y.M.C.A. = Young, Masculine, Comradery Athletics

36) Y.W.C.A. = Young Women's Creative Associates

37) F.B.I. = Friggin' Bunch of … Just Kidding. Actually I hold the FBI in highest esteem. F.B.I. = Fabulous Band of Intelligence and Intuition

38) A.A. = Among Angels

39) P.T.A. = Partially Talented Associates

40) If you smoke, it's likely to be something you rolled yourself or fits just fine in a pipe.

41) Daylight Savings Time is just a pain in the ass and you wish "they" would leave the clocks to hell alone!

42) Is it true that your "so called" black sheep of the family is actually quite flashy and you're even more than a bit proud of 'em.

43) Have you noticed that all your summer clothes fit in the closet and dresser WITH your winter clothes?

44) Maybe, many of your summer clothes ARE your winter clothes.

It was suggested to me that these last few may be more appropriate for males. But, go ahead ladies and have at em – give it a go. There are pretty hearty, intelligent women all over this country.

45) Sayings like "Love those winta beaters" and "If that doesn't just suck like a tit through a flannel nightie" are part of your day to day conversation.

46) A "winta beatuh" is a car or truck that is just hung together enough to get you through the winter without dying.

47) Do you like your companion to have that "extra healthy", sturdy look and NOT that spindly, wear out fast, might-break-a-nail-choppin'-wood look?

48) When you're asked if you've seen any "chicks" lately, you assume they're talking about some kind of birds.

49) You believe a prime body is one on four wheels and just needs a few finished coats.

50) If you have ANY bumper stickers, you make sure (sho-uh) they're <u>wicked</u> important, knowing they'll be there for <u>ONE LONG TIME.</u>

51) Do you find terms like "shit head", "asshole", "bastard", and "son of a bitch" can double as words of approval, or affection, depending on the situation AND inflection?

52) Come winter (wintah), you make sure you keep extra antifreeze for the automobile <u>behind</u> the seat and extra antifreeze for yourself under the seat. Otherwise known as four on the floor and a 5th under the seat! NOTE: These are for emergencies only. We don't condone drinkin' and' drivin'.

Now, total your points and see what you find (one point for ay-uh, NO points for uh-uh, 1/2 point for probly [short for probably])

Wicked Official Down Eastah Test Results
50 - 30 = a True Wicked Official Down Eastah
29 - 18 = could pass for a local
below 18 = definitely from away

If you didn't qualify the first time, why not try the bonus questions?

1) Your good friends can visit any time – even if they're too darn thick to take a hint when it's time to leave.

2) Your idea of a subtle hint for someone to leave is to go to the door, open it, and thank 'em for stoppin' by.

3) <u>You </u>never take offense at a "subtle" hint 'cause you know they're too darn good to hurt anyone's feelings on purpose.

4) You know "the little woman" has become more fashion conscious when she traded in her polyester pants with snags for sweatpants or overalls/jeans.

5) When you're <u>way</u> down, that is lower than whale shit, a quiet, steady trickle of strength comes from somewhere deep inside (or from above) and gives you a jump-start for dealin' with life.

6) Your good breedin' shows. You have house rules and all are welcome as long as they abide by those rules.

7) When you hear of a full blown Nor Eastah or Sow Westah comin', you know it's <u>serious </u>and try not to let on how excited you are.

8) With the storm comin', you know stayin' in is the sound-minded thing to do,but ya just can't resist going down to check out the wind and waves – at Thunder Hole, especially.

9) As it turns out, the "black sheep" of your family is really quite creative and even a bit philosophical.

10) As the wind whips at you on the shore and the spray becomes the air, you're awed by the tremendous power of it all and sense the essence of a sea lover's dream. Humbled yet?

What did you discover? It all goes to prove one thing – you're probably a TRUE Wicked Official Down Eastah, even if it is "just" at heart.